OUS STUDIES GCSE

AQA B

Thinking about God and Morality

14-07

Marianne Fleming

heinemann.co.uk
✓ Free online support
✓ Useful weblinks
✓ 24 hour online ordering

01865 888058

Heinemann Educational Publishers
Halley Court, Jordan Hill, Oxford OX2 8EJ
Part of Harcourt Education

Heinemann is the registered trademark of Harcourt Education Limited

© Marianne Fleming, 2003

First published 2003

08 07 06
10 9 8 7 6 5 4

British Library Cataloguing in Publication Data is available from the British Library on request.

10-digit ISBN: 0 435 307 00 2
13-digit ISBN: 978 0 435 307 00 4

Copyright notice
All rights reserved. No part of this publication may be reproduced in any form or by any means (including photocopying or storing it in any medium by electronic means and whether or not transiently or incidentally to some other use of this publication) without the written permission of the copyright owner, except in accordance with the provisions of the Copyright, Designs and Patents Act 1988 or under the terms of a licence issued by the Copyright Licensing Agency, 90 Tottenham Court Road, London W1T 4LP. Applications for the copyright owner's written permission should be addressed to the publisher.

Designed by Artistix
Typeset by TechType, Abingdon, Oxon

Original illustrations © Harcourt Education Limited, 2003

Illustrated by TechType, Abingdon, Oxon
Printed in the UK by CPI Bath
Cover photo © Getty

Acknowledgements
The publishers would like to thank the following for the use of their logos on pp. 45–6:
© Christian Aid (2003), used with permission;
© CAFOD; © Trócaire; © Tearfund; © Tzedek;
© Muslim Aid; ©ISKCON; © Karuna Trust;
© Khalsa Aid.

The publishers would like to thank the following for permission to reproduce photographs: p. 14 (top two) Alamy; p. 14 Getty; p. 21 Andes Press Agency; pp. 27, 35, 36, 39 Corbis; p. 49 (top) Camera Press; p. 49 (middle) Hulton Getty; p. 59 SPL.

p. 18 artwork adapted from *Christianity in Today's World: Moral Issues, Ultimate Questions* (John Murray, 1998) by Clinton, Lynch, Orchard, Weston and Wright, reproduced by permission of Hodder Murray.

Every effort has been made to contact copyright holders of material reproduced in this book. Any omissions will be rectified in subsequent printings if notice is given to the publishers.

Websites
There are links to relevant websites in this book. In order to ensure that the links are up-to-date, that the links work, and that the sites are not inadvertently linked to sites that could be considered offensive, we have made the links available on the Heinemann website at www.heinemann.co.uk/hotlinks. When you access the site, enter the express code **7002P**, and this will take you to the links you want.

Tel: 01865 888058 www.heinemann.co.uk

Contents

How to use this book   4

Section A: Thinking about God

1. The existence of God   6
2. The problem of suffering   13
3. The problem of evil   18
4. The nature of God   21

Section B: Thinking about morality

5. Ways of making moral decisions   25
6. Abortion   27
7. Sex, marriage and divorce   32
8. Prejudice and discrimination   38
9. World poverty   43
10. War and peace   48
11. The natural world   55

Glossary   62

Index   64

How to use this book

Thinking about God and morality is one of the most important things we can do because it makes us examine people's deepest beliefs and values. Philosophers have asked questions about the meaning and purpose of life for centuries. This module allows you to argue about these questions, to find out what religions teach about them, and to form your own 'philosophy of life'.

Which religious tradition?

You are expected to study most of these questions through Christianity and *one* other religious tradition. In this book, Christianity is used for any topics that require only *one* religious tradition since it has to be studied by everyone.

If you studied Christianity only, you must show that Christians have different attitudes to particular issues. Even if you mainly studied two religions, it may help to refer to a third for certain topics. For example, Hindu beliefs about the nature of God or vegetarianism are distinctive and will allow you to bring out a contrasting point of view in your answers.

However, do not use more than *two* religions in answer to any one question and no more than *three* in the paper as a whole.

Your course

Module 1 has two sections. In Section A, Thinking about God, you must refer to *one* religious tradition to answer questions on these topics:

- arguments for and against God's existence
- the problem of suffering
- the problem of evil.

You must refer to *two* religious traditions to answer questions on this topic:

- the nature of God (what God is like).

In Section B, Thinking about Morality, you must know the attitudes and beliefs of *two* religious traditions, one of which must be Christianity, for each of these issues:

- abortion
- sex, marriage and divorce
- prejudice and discrimination
- world poverty
- war and peace
- the natural world.

Part of Section B is called 'Ways of making moral decisions'. You must know:

- the meaning of absolute and relative morality
- what religious believers use as sources of moral authority
- how religious beliefs affect people's behaviour.

The exam paper

You must answer *four* questions, each worth 20 marks, in one hour and 45 minutes.

Section A: one stimulus-based short answer question; one essay question.

Section B: one question from two of these topics: abortion, sex, marriage and divorce, or prejudice and discrimination, and one question from two of these topics: world poverty, war and peace, or the natural world.

Some questions may make reference to more than one topic.

Quotations

Learn two or three quotations from sacred texts or general religious principles and, if appropriate, one statement or teaching by a religious leader or authority. Some examples will be given in this book, but you should use the ones you have spent two years studying. Do not waste time trying to learn unfamiliar texts.

How this book is organized

Each section begins with 'What do I need to know?' which outlines information you will need to answer examination questions on the topic.

Margin features

Did you know?
Short pieces of information that are useful additions to your knowledge and can be used as examples in examination answers.

Hints and tips
Brief guidelines designed to assist revision and examination technique.

Exam watch
Brief tips to help you achieve better marks in your exam.

Beware
Tips to help you avoid commonly made mistakes in the exam.

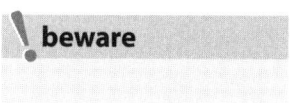

Key ideas
Short points that summarize the main points in a section.

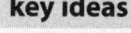

Action point
Brief exercise that you can practise to help you revise.

Read more
Suggestions for further reading to help you add more

detail to your answers. These may also direct you to another section of the book where passages or topics are explained in more detail.

Key words

Important words and terms are in bold print the first time they appear in the book. Definitions can be found in the Glossary on pages 62–3. You should learn these and be prepared to explain them.

Questions

Each section ends with practice questions with the number of marks in brackets. This guides how much you should write.

Mark	Requirement
1	Write a simple one-word answer or a short sentence
2	'Give *two* reasons…' = write two simple points 'Explain…' = make one simple point with a sentence to explain it
3	Make one simple point, explain it and give an example
4 or more	Write continuously (see below)

Questions worth 4 marks or more are usually marked on levels of response. The examiner decides which level you reached in your answer and awards the marks attached to that level.

Questions worth 5 marks (evaluation questions) usually begin with a controversial statement and ask, 'Do you agree? Give reasons for your answer, showing that you have thought about more than one point of view.' Some also say, 'Refer to religious teachings in your answer.' These are always marked on levels of response. You cannot reach Levels 4 and 5 unless you refer to more than one point of view. You cannot reach Level 5 without referring to at least one religious teaching.

SECTION A: THINKING ABOUT GOD

1 The existence of God

What do I need to know?

- Origins of the universe: **creation** or random chance?
- The **Big Bang** theory.
- The theory of **evolution**.
- A creation story from a religious **tradition**.
- The **First Cause** argument.
- Arguments for and against the **design argument**.
- Religious experience: illusion or reality?
- Types of **religious experience**: **conversion**, **sacramental ritual**, **charismatic worship**, **prayer** and **meditation**.
- The meaning of: **theist**, **atheist** and **agnostic**.

hints and tips
You need only refer to *one* religious tradition in this section.

People who believe that God exists are called theists.

People who believe that God does not exist are called atheists.

People who believe that we can only know about material things so it is impossible to know whether a God exists or not are called agnostics.

did you know?
Most of the world's religions (except for Buddhism) believe in a creator God.

The Big Bang theory

- 15,000 million years ago matter was concentrated into a tiny, dense mass and then expanded with the speed and force of an explosion. It continues to expand today.
- All planets, stars and matter come from the gathering and cooling of matter sent out by the big bang.

Evolution

Evolution is:

- natural selection by survival of the fittest
- when species change by adapting to their environment.

Life began in the sea. Over time species have changed from simple to complex creatures: jellyfish, fish, amphibians, reptiles, mammals, apes, and eventually humans. This process took hundreds of millions of years.

key ideas
Theists believe that God created the universe and life on earth for a purpose and that it was not made by accident or chance. They believe that human beings are special because they are made in God's image and have a special **responsibility** for God's creation.

The First Cause argument (St Thomas Aquinas)

- The universe itself is the best evidence for God.
- Everything in the world has a cause, so the universe must also have a cause.

1 The existence of God

- There had to be something eternal (without beginning or end) that was not caused by anything.
- God is that eternal first cause.

A modern way of putting this is that God caused the big bang that started the universe and eventually all life evolved from it.

Arguments against God as the first cause

- Just because events or things have causes, it does not mean the universe itself has a cause.
- The universe could have always existed (be eternal), so there is no need for anything or anyone else to bring it into being.
- The first cause still does not answer 'who or what caused God?'
- A 'first cause' does not seem to match what believers mean by a **personal** God.

A creation story from a religious tradition

The seven-day story (Genesis 1–2: 4)

 **Day 1** *Light and dark (day and night)*

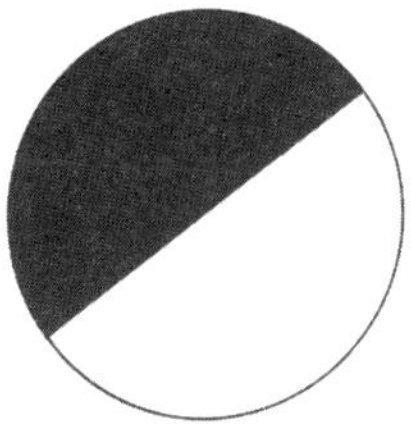

Day 2 *Sky*

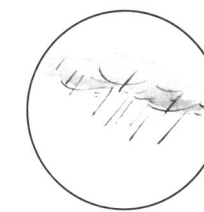 **Day 3** *Land, sea and plants*

Day 4 *Sun, moon and stars*

 **Day 5** *Fish and birds*

 **Day 6** *Animals and human beings, both male and female*

God rested

Day 7

> **exam watch**
> You will not lose marks by mentioning Adam and Eve or the Garden of Eden, but make sure you write *the entire* seven-day story first!

> **beware**
> If you use the Adam and Eve story, be sure to stop at their creation. Do not go on to describe the Fall (Genesis 3). This is not about creation but explains how suffering and death came into the world.

You must know one creation story in detail. To gain full marks you need to state clearly the name of the religious tradition your story comes from (for example, Christianity); what was created each day; that God created the universe from nothing and that God saw that the creation was good, a perfect creation.

> **did you know?**
> The creation story in Islam (Adam and Hawa) is very similar to the story of Adam and Eve. It is in the Qur'an, surah 2: 30–9.
>
>

Can you believe in evolution and in a creator God?

No	Yes
• Evolution says humans came from apes, not from the soil and a man's rib. • Evolution took many hundreds of millions of years, not seven days. • The process of natural selection was not guided by a God; it was just luck or chance that the strong survived over the weak.	• Creation stories are not 'scientific'. They show how people tried to make sense of their purpose and place in the world, and its great beauty and majesty. • Most believers accept evolution, even though it has not been proved, but God could still have created the conditions for evolution to take place. • It was such a unique event that just the right conditions existed for life to begin on earth that it could not have been an accident and must have had a purposeful power behind it – God.

The design of the universe

Some people believe that nature is so intricate and complex that God must have designed it. It could not have happened by random chance.

Sir Isaac Newton's thumb

The human thumb's design is so clever and unique to every individual that it alone convinced Newton that there was a designer of the world.

William Paley's watch

William Paley compared the world to a watch found lying on the ground. If you had never seen a watch before, its intricate workings would convince you that it was designed. Cogs, wheels and springs could not have come together by themselves.

The universe is even more complicated than the watch. For example, the human eye is more complex than a telescope, which can only help the eye. Therefore, the universe must have had a designer – God.

Arguments against a designer

- Evolution: since the process of natural selection (the fittest survive, the rest die out) happens by chance, species really designed themselves.

> **✓ action point**
> Write a sentence to explain how each of these shows good 'design':
> • a snowflake
> • the human body
> • nature itself.

1 The existence of God

But even in Darwin's day, people argued that God had started evolution knowing how it would turn out. Human beings, with such high powers of intellect and the capacity to create and be moved by great music, art and literature, could not arrive at such complexity entirely by chance.

- Design faults: if God designed the world, why are there so many faults in its structure (plates in the earth's crust move causing earthquakes, and so on)? The universe has always existed and continues to develop and change.
- The problem of evil: if God designed everyone and everything, why did God create evil? Why is nature so cruel?

See the section on suffering, pages 13–17.

See the section on evil, pages 18–20.

Religious experience

Many people believe in God because they say they have experienced God personally in their lives.

Conversion

A conversion (change of belief) can convince people of God's love and protection. It is usually deeply personal, unique to each individual and life changing.

Sacramental ritual

 A **sacrament** is an outward (religious) action that gives a spiritual blessing to those involved. A sacramental ritual is any religious service or ceremony that follows a set pattern in which a sacrament is celebrated. Liturgical worship comes into this category.

Roman Catholic and Orthodox Christians accept seven sacraments	Most Protestant Christians and Anglicans accept two sacraments
• Baptism	• Baptism
• Sacrament of Reconciliation (Penance)	• Holy Communion
• Holy Communion (the Eucharist)	
• Confirmation	
• Matrimony (marriage)	
• Holy Orders (Ordination)	
• Sacrament of the Sick (Anointing or Holy Unction)	

Sacraments help believers because they make the invisible, untouchable God more real. For example, when Christians receive Holy Communion (bread and wine symbolizing the body and blood of Jesus Christ) they feel God's real presence inside them physically.

Charismatic experiences and worship

 Some Christian worship is charismatic, meaning 'filled with and led by the Holy Spirit'. The first Christians experienced the Holy Spirit on the Day of Pentecost (Acts 2). They were given spiritual gifts of prophesying and speaking in 'tongues' (strange languages or sounds that seem to pour out of the person).

hints and tips

People say God has been revealed to them through such experiences. See **special revelation**, pages 22–23.

action point

You should learn *one* example of a conversion. In the Bible, Moses (Exodus 3: 1–17) experienced God in a burning bush and St Paul (Acts 9: 1–19) was blinded on the road to Damascus. There are many modern examples. Write down the main points of the account you choose.

9

Features of charismatic worship	How it affects the worshipper
• Singing • Praying aloud • Speaking in tongues • Raising arms in the air • Uncontrollable laughter, tears, shaking, and so on	• New awareness of God's presence and power • Direct communication with God • Communicating God to others • Feeling saved from sin; surrendering to God's will • Feeling changed or touched by God's Holy Spirit

Prayer and meditation

Prayer is talking to God aloud or silently, in public or in private. There are prayers of praise, thanksgiving, confessing sins and asking for things for oneself or others.

Meditation is being in God's presence, silently focusing on God, pushing all distractions from one's mind. Sometimes a phrase is repeated over and over (a mantra). Passages from **scripture** are used so the person can think deeply about their meaning. Others feel God becomes present to them when they focus fully on a simple activity like washing up.

Effects of prayer and meditation

Some people believe that prayer can help them feel closer to a personal, **immanent** God (see page 21). By talking to God as a friend, the relationship grows. Placing all problems in the hands of someone more powerful brings comfort and strength to cope with whatever life brings.

Meditation can help someone feel that God is real. By opening the mind and heart and really listening, a believer can receive a revelation of God's peace and love. Some people claim they have had visions while meditating. This convinces them of the reality of God.

Other kinds of religious experiences include visions, dreams and miracles (see special revelation, pages 22–23).

Are such experiences illusion or reality?

An atheist or an agnostic would say that such experiences are illusions (imaginary, not real) and are not good evidence for God's existence.

- Private experiences have no reliable outside witnesses.
- Public worship can be observed but it is impossible to be certain what it is people are experiencing.
- It could be a psychological phenomenon, imagination, mass hysteria, a trick of the mind, wishful thinking or hallucinations.
- Miracles have no apparent natural explanation but this does not mean that they were brought about by God.
- If someone said God spoke to them in a dream, you could say they dreamed God spoke to them, a very different matter.
- In an extreme case, the person might be lying or making the experience up.

1 The existence of God

A theist would argue that religious experiences are real and are good evidence for God's existence.

- Conversion really changes a person. Its effects can be observed by others.
- Prayer, meditation and **sacramental worship** have a deep impact on those who practise them. To them they are real experiences of God.
- Charismatic worship is sometimes quite dramatic. Its effects can also be seen in believers' lives.
- Visions and dreams are very real to the person who experiences them. If God is within each person, He could inspire them to dream about God.
- Some healing miracles have been verified by doctors. The people who have been healed know that what happened to them was real.

Luke 24: 13–49.

Short questions

a What is an atheist? (1 mark)
b What is a theist? (1 mark)
c What is an agnostic? (1 mark)
d What is charismatic worship? Give an example. (2 marks)
e Give one example of sacramental worship. (1 mark)

Using bullet points is fine for revision, but you will lose marks if you use them in the exam.

Examination type questions

a Outline the argument for the existence of God based on design of the universe. (4 marks) (NEAB, 1999)
b Explain why some people think the world is a result of chance. (4 marks) (NEAB, 1999)

Student's answer

a *Some people say the world must have been designed by God because nature is so beautiful and complex. William Paley said that the world was like a watch found lying on the ground. Even if you had never seen a watch before, you could see that it had been designed because the little parts could not have been put together by accident. The world is even more complicated than a watch.*

b *People think the world is the result of chance because they do not think it shows that it was designed by anyone. Why would a designer make a world where so many things go wrong, like earthquakes and volcanoes, which kill innocent people? Also, in nature, a lot of animals destroy each other and life is wasted. Evolution is just a matter of luck. The fittest survive and the rest die. So the way we are is just the way humans have adapted to survive.*

Examiner's comments

a A good answer, accurately telling Paley's argument, but it stops abruptly without concluding 'therefore the only being capable of designing such a complex universe is God.' No mention of Newton's thumb or comparison of the eye with a telescope or any examples of the beauty or complexity of nature.

Mark: 3/4

b Excellent answer incorporating design flaws, the cruelty of nature and evolution as an explanation for complexity.

Mark: 4/4

Examination practice

a **i** What is the Big Bang theory? (2 marks) (AQA, 2002)
   ii What is the theory of evolution? (2 marks) (AQA, 2002)

b **i** Give an account of a creation story from a religious tradition. (6 marks) (AQA, 2002)
   ii How might believing that God created the world affect the way people think about life and themselves? (5 marks) (AQA, 2002)

c 'Scientific theories about the origins of the universe prove there is no God.' Do you agree? Give reasons for your answer, showing that you have thought about more than one point of view. (5 marks) (AQA, 2002)

Checklist for revision

	Understand and know	Need more revision	Do not understand
I know and understand the Big Bang theory.	☐	☐	☐
I know and understand the theory of evolution.	☐	☐	☐
I know *one* creation story in detail.	☐	☐	☐
I understand why some people say you can and others say you cannot believe in *both* evolution *and* a creator God.	☐	☐	☐
I know and understand the First Cause argument.	☐	☐	☐
I understand why some people are not convinced by the First Cause argument.	☐	☐	☐
I know the arguments for God's existence based on design of the universe.	☐	☐	☐
I know at least *two* arguments against the design argument.	☐	☐	☐
I understand the view that the universe began by random chance.	☐	☐	☐
I understand the meaning of the terms:			
• theist	☐	☐	☐
• atheist	☐	☐	☐
• agnostic.	☐	☐	☐
I know the argument for God's existence based on religious experience.	☐	☐	☐
I understand why some people think religious experiences are illusions.	☐	☐	☐
I understand and can give an example of:			
• conversion	☐	☐	☐
• sacramental ritual	☐	☐	☐
• charismatic worship	☐	☐	☐
• prayer	☐	☐	☐
• meditation.	☐	☐	☐

SECTION A: THINKING ABOUT GOD

2 The problem of suffering

What do I need to know?
- What questions does suffering raise about God's love and purposes?
- In what ways is suffering unjust?
- Types of suffering: natural or man-made?
- Does suffering have a purpose?
- The meaning of **free will**.
- Religious responses to suffering.

hints and tips
You need only refer to *one* religious tradition in this section.

Suffering is a 'problem' for everyone. We all suffer no matter how lucky we are. Human beings experience pain, illness, loss, and finally death.

But suffering is called a 'problem' here because it is a problem for believers in an all-good, all-loving, all-powerful, all-knowing God. It makes people question God's love, God's purpose (will) and God's power.

Questions raised by suffering
- Why is there so much suffering in the world?
- Is it God's intention (purpose) to make us suffer? (If so, then God must be cruel.) Or does suffering just occur without God wanting it to happen? (If so, then God must be weak.)
- If God is all-loving and cares for us, why does God allow us to suffer? (If God wants us to suffer then God is not loving, God is cruel.)
- If God is all-powerful, God must be able to stop our suffering, yet suffering continues. (If God cannot stop our suffering then God is not powerful, God is weak.)
- If God is all-knowing, God must realize we suffer. Surely God's knowledge and power could be used to stop suffering? Why is it not?

How is suffering unjust?
Innocent suffering: people who have lived good lives or children who have not done anything wrong do not deserve to suffer.

Types of suffering: natural or man-made?

Does suffering have a purpose?
- Not all suffering is pointless – pain tells us something is wrong with us so we can do something about it.
- Some people say suffering has made them a better or stronger person.

✓ action point
Write down *three* examples of suffering that you think are unfair or undeserved. Why was the suffering in each case unjust?

13

> **action point**
> Which pictures show natural suffering and which show suffering caused by people? Give a reason for each choice.

- Some suffer to achieve a goal, for example, a mountain climber or polar explorer.
- Some suffering helps others, for example, self-sacrifice during war.
- Suffering may be a test of a person's faith.
- Suffering may teach a lesson (it used to be thought it was a punishment for sin).
- Suffering may have a purpose (be part of God's plan) but we do not know what that purpose is.

Religious responses to suffering

Buddhism

- The Buddha taught that life is unsatisfactory, full of suffering (dukkha).
- The cause of suffering is desire.
- The cure is to overcome desire by following the 'Middle Way' set out in the 'Eightfold Path'– a path that leads to escape (nibbana).

Christianity

- The story of the Fall (Genesis 3) explains that suffering and evil came into God's perfect creation because of human disobedience. Adam and Eve then had to face the consequences of their free choice.
- Christians believe that natural suffering is not God's fault – just part of the way the world has developed since its creation by God.
- Suffering caused by human beings occurs because God gave people free will.
- Christians believe Jesus made up for the sins of humans by his innocent suffering and death on the cross, so breaking the power of evil and suffering over humans.
- Trusting in God helps Christians to endure suffering.
- Christians accept personal suffering as God's (mysterious) will but they will try to alleviate the suffering of others whenever they can.

key ideas

People are free to choose how to behave and sometimes choose actions that cause suffering.

Hinduism

- Suffering is the result of sin in this life and in previous lives.
- People reap what they sow (karma).
- Building up good karma will reduce future suffering and achieve release (moksha).

Islam

- Allah gave Adam free will so humans can choose to sin.
- Satan (Iblis) was given the job of testing human faith.
- Suffering tests faith and character.
- Muslims should show **compassion** towards those suffering. (One of the 99 names of Allah is 'The Compassionate'.)
- If people cause suffering they will be judged on the Day of Judgement.

Judaism

- Suffering results from free will.
- Adam and Eve brought suffering into the world by their disobedience to God (Genesis 3).
- Jews suffered terribly through the Holocaust.
- Jews are encouraged to help those who suffer.
- God uses suffering to discipline His people (Deuteronomy 8: 5) and to bring people back to Him (Isaiah 53: 5).
- The book of Job gives three explanations for his suffering: it is a test of faith, a punishment for sin (which God rejects), and part of God's purpose (beyond human understanding).

Sikhism

- Selfishness causes suffering.
- Actions in the physical world affect rebirth so it is important to do good.
- Suffering is the result of karma.
- It is the aim to rise beyond or transcend suffering.
- Some suffering is a mystery including why people suffer more in some parts of the world than in others.

Short questions

a Write down *two* different questions about God which are raised by suffering in the world.
(2 marks) (NEAB, 1999)

b Explain how religious believers can respond in a positive way to suffering. (2 marks) (NEAB, 1999)

Examination type questions

a What problems are raised for religious believers by suffering? (4 marks) (NEAB, 1998)

b Explain how believing in God can help people to cope with suffering in their lives.
(6 marks) (NEAB, 1998)

c 'Without suffering and evil in the world, people would not turn to God to become better people.' Do you agree? Give reasons for your answer, showing that you have thought about more than one point of view. (5 marks) (NEAB, 1998)

Student's answer

a Suffering makes people question whether God really exists. People say God is all-loving. If God loves us, why would He deliberately make us suffer? How can He stand by and let a child die?

b Someone who believes in God will feel that God is listening to their prayers. This brings them comfort. Their faith in God will give them strength to cope with the pain they are going through. If he or she is a Christian, they will know that Jesus suffered too and this will help knowing they are not alone. If someone they love is dying, they will believe that God will bring them into his kingdom and they will be at peace.

c I agree. People who have never suffered usually feel they do not need God. They have everything they want without God, so why bother believing in him? Many people turn to God in a crisis. But I also disagree, because many people believe in God and live good lives whether they have suffered or not. Also, it would be hard to tell a mother who just lost her baby that it was all right because God was just trying to make her a better person. That just makes God sound cruel.

Examiner's comments

a A good explanation of one of the questions raised – whether God can be all-loving and allow suffering. However, no mention was made of the challenge to God's power or omniscience that suffering raises.
Mark: 2/4

b An excellent explanation of the effects of faith in God on a person who suffers, with four points made, two of which were developed.
Mark: 6/6

c Excellent evaluation with both sides considered and developed.
Mark: 5/5

Checklist for revision

	Understand and know	Need more revision	Do not understand
I understand why suffering is a problem for believers in God.	☐	☐	☐
I know the question suffering raises about God's love.	☐	☐	☐
I know the question suffering raises about God's purpose (intention).	☐	☐	☐
I know the question suffering raises about God's power.	☐	☐	☐
I know why suffering is unjust and can give examples.	☐	☐	☐
I know the difference between natural suffering and suffering caused by human beings, and I can give some examples of each.	☐	☐	☐
I understand why believers use this difference to argue that suffering is not God's fault.	☐	☐	☐
I know at least *three* ways in which suffering can be said to have a purpose (or even a positive benefit).	☐	☐	☐
I know the meaning of free will.	☐	☐	☐
I know and understand how religious people explain suffering.	☐	☐	☐
I can give examples of how religious people respond to their own personal suffering.	☐	☐	☐
I can give examples of how religious people respond to the suffering of others.	☐	☐	☐
I understand how religious faith can help people face suffering.	☐	☐	☐

SECTION A: THINKING ABOUT GOD

3 The problem of evil

What do I need to know?

- Where does evil come from? (One religious explanation for its origin.)
- What is its nature – an impersonal force, a personal being or a psychological phenomenon?
- What questions does the existence of evil raise about God's creation and power?
- Religious responses to the problem of evil.

hints and tips
You need only refer to *one* religious tradition in this section.

hints and tips
The problem of evil is closely connected to the problem of suffering. See pages 13–17.

Where does evil come from?

Here are some different ideas about what evil is and where it comes from.

- It comes from God (by giving humans free will).
- It comes from human nature (greed, selfishness, lack of respect, and so on).
- It is an impersonal force that draws people into choosing the wrong path.
- It is a personal being who tempts people to sin (the devil, Satan, Shaytan).
- It is a psychological phenomenon (a damaged mind or influenced by a person's upbringing and society).

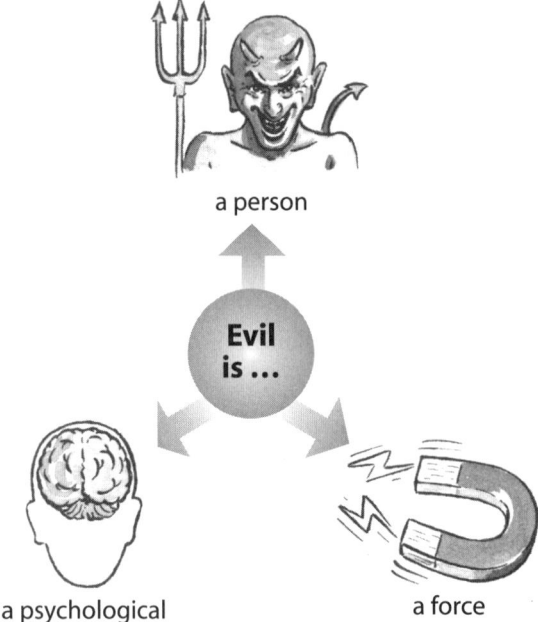

Religious explanations for the origin of evil

Buddhists do not believe in an all-powerful God so evil does not raise the same questions for them as it does for other religious traditions. They believe that evil is caused by the selfish desires of people. Doing good can overcome evil.

Hindus believe that the cycle of birth, death and rebirth (samsara) is a 'natural' evil, but people also act immorally. Good actions can make up for evil actions in this or a previous life (the law of karma).

hints and tips
Religious explanations of the origin of evil are closely linked to understanding of suffering. See pages 13–17.

3 The problem of evil

Christians believe evil came into the world as a result of Adam and Eve's disobedience (original sin). It occurs when people use their free will to disobey God. People want to be good but they are tempted to do wrong. They need salvation (rescuing) from sin.

Jews believe that evil is a result of the free will God gave humans (see Genesis 3). God wants people to act justly, be merciful, and walk humbly with God (Micah 6: 8). People can choose to reject God.

Muslims believe Shaytan, the source of evil, tries to turn people away from Allah. Evildoers will be called to account and punished on the Day of Judgement. Allah is merciful and compassionate, so those who truly repent will be forgiven.

Sikhs believe people are not evil by nature, but they are ignorant and self-centred (haumai). This prevents them from realizing the truth and doing good. God is the source of everything, both good and evil. People are given free will to choose between them.

See Genesis 3 for how evil entered the world in the Bible. This gives a detailed account of one religious explanation.

Questions raised about God's creation and power

- Why did God create a world in which evil is possible?
- If God is all-powerful, why can God not prevent someone from doing evil? Since evil continues, God does not seem to be able to stop it (God is not all-powerful).

See also the problem of suffering, pages 13–17.

Religious responses to the problem of evil

- God gave us free will to choose good or evil.
- The fact that God made us free (and not robots) shows God's love.
- God is powerful but chooses not to use that power; for example, God allowed Jesus to die on the cross.

Essay questions often combine the problems of suffering and evil.

Examination practice

a Give *two* examples of suffering caused by nature. (2 marks) (NEAB, 2001)

b Outline the teaching of *one* religious tradition about suffering. (5 marks) (NEAB, 2001)

c Give *two* explanations for the origin of evil. (4 marks) (NEAB, 2001)

d Explain why the existence of evil raises problems for people who believe in God. (4 marks) (NEAB, 2001)

e 'The fact that people suffer has nothing to do with God.' Do you agree? Give reasons for your answer, showing that you have thought about more than one point of view. (5 marks) (NEAB, 2001)

Checklist for revision

	Understand and know	Need more revision	Do not understand
I know *one* religious explanation of how evil entered the world (for example, the Fall in Genesis 3).	☐	☐	☐
I know *three* explanations of evil:			
• as an impersonal force	☐	☐	☐
• as a personal being	☐	☐	☐
• as a psychological phenomenon.	☐	☐	☐
I know the questions the existence of evil raises about:			
• God's creation	☐	☐	☐
• God's power.	☐	☐	☐
I know how religious people respond to each of these questions.	☐	☐	☐

SECTION A: THINKING ABOUT GOD

4 The nature of God

What do I need to know?

- How God is understood (in *two* religious traditions or different views within one tradition).
- Is God personal or **impersonal**?
- Is God immanent or **transcendent**?
- Is God 'One' or does God have many different 'aspects' or 'forms'?
- The meaning of **monotheism** and **polytheism**.
- Can God be known? If so, how?
- The difference between **general revelation** and special revelation and examples of each.

hints and tips
In this section you must refer to *two* religious traditions or different views within the same religion. Christians, for example, think of God as personal and impersonal, immanent and transcendent, and as One God in three persons: Father, Son and Holy Spirit.

The 'nature' of God means what God is like or how people understand God. Even atheists have some idea of God that they reject!

Christians understand God as a supreme being who created all things. They describe God as good, loving, just, powerful and merciful, appearing to give God human characteristics (personal). They think of God as close to people, involved in the world, acting in human history (immanent), yet they know this limits God. They also think God is beyond human understanding, eternal, all-knowing, mysterious, more like a force (impersonal) and not limited by time or space, outside the world, taking no active part in human life (transcendent). They believe God is One (monotheism) but they speak of the Trinity (God the Father, God the Son, and God the Holy Spirit).

Hindus understand God as the atman (soul), which lives in each person (personal and immanent), but also as Brahman, without form, the source of all life, outside human experience and understanding, the energy that keeps the universe in being (impersonal and transcendent). Brahman cannot be fully known but the images or deities show many sides to Brahman's nature (for example, Vishnu, the preserving, and Shiva, the destructive, aspects of Brahman) and make God more personal to the believer.

did you know?
These qualities seem contradictory, but Christians emphasize some more than others and many think you need all of them to do justice to their idea of God. All theists share many of these ideas.

did you know?
Avatars (God taking on human forms) also help Hindus relate to the supreme spirit in a personal way.

Think about the following questions.

- Personal: how can God be everywhere at the same time, care for everyone, answer prayers, if God is just a person?
- Impersonal: how can people have a meaningful relationship with a 'force' or impersonal 'spirit', or prime number (One), or the idea of infinity, or some other idea in the minds of people?
- Immanent: if God is 'in the world' does that mean God is *part* of the world? How then did God create it?
- Transcendent: if God is remote and separate from human existence, how can people relate to God? Can God be both immanent and transcendent?

One or many forms?

In ancient times, some people were polytheists, believing in many gods: a god of war, a god of storms, fertility gods, and so on. Now all religions (except Buddhism, which does not believe in a God) accept that God is One. God cannot be divided up. Yet Christians speak about three persons in God and Hindus have different deities, which show different aspects of God. Is it more helpful to believers to think of God as 'One' than to think of different 'aspects' of God or of several different gods?

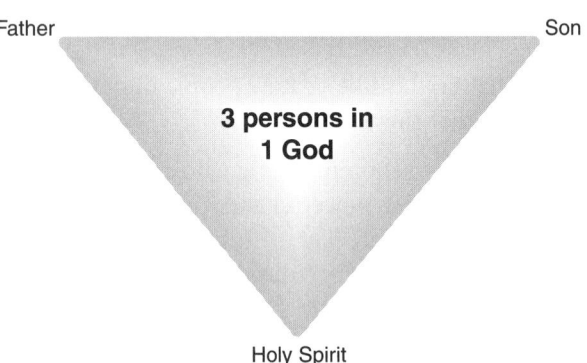

Can God be known? If so, how?

God cannot be known

- We can only truly 'know' things we can see, touch, taste, feel and smell. God cannot be 'known' in this way.
- God is greater than everything that exists. It is impossible for the created intelligence of humans to fully understand God.
- God cannot be described adequately in pictures or words. Metaphors and symbols are all that is possible. Human language limits God. When Moses asks God's name, the answer is obscure: 'I am who I am.' (Exodus 3: 14)
- Certain qualities of God may be understood or perceived but never God in all God's 'holiness' or 'otherness'.
- God is pure mystery and therefore cannot be known.

General and special revelation

Religious believers say that God *can* be known or that God is 'revealed' through:

- nature
- religious writings
- personal experience.
- the lives and work of religious leaders
- formal or informal worship

---

action point

Write *two* sentences to explain each idea about God: personal, impersonal, immanent and transcendent. First give a definition, then give an example or further explanation.

beware

Hindus are *not* polytheists (believing in more than one god). Hindus believe God has different aspects, represented by the different images of the deities, but they believe that God is One (monotheists).

action point

Write *two* reasons why some people prefer to think of God as immanent. How do they show this belief in their worship?

action point

Write *two* reasons why some people prefer to think of God as transcendent. Give an example of how they show this belief in their worship.

The difference between general and special revelation

General revelation	Special revelation
• Indirect	• Direct
• Available to everyone	• Available to an individual or group
• Describes experiencing God through the natural world, reason, conscience or moral sense	• Describes experiencing God through a dream, vision, prophecy, special event (miracle?) or personal experience

Short questions

a Explain how nature can reveal God. (2 marks) (NEAB, 2000)

b Is finding God in nature an example of general revelation or special revelation? Give a reason for your answer. (2 marks) (NEAB, 2000)

c Many people believe that they experience God through worship. State *two* kinds of worship which help some people to experience God. (2 marks) (NEAB, 2000)

d What might believers learn about God from *one* of these kinds of worship? (2 marks) (NEAB, 2000)

e Explain the difference between 'general revelation' and 'special revelation'. Use examples from *two* religious traditions. (4 marks) (NEAB, 1999)

f Explain why some people say that all forms of revelation are illusions and not real. (4 marks) (NEAB, 1999)

Examination type question

'Human beings cannot understand God.' Do you agree? Give reasons for your answer, showing that you have thought about more than one point of view. (5 marks) (AQA, 2002)

Student's answer

I disagree because I am a Christian. We can understand God because God shows Himself to us through His Son, Jesus. God showed His great love for us by giving us His only Son who died for our sins on the cross. This helps us understand that God cares for us and wants us to live forever with Him in heaven. Jesus is God so we can know how God wants us to live by following his example. On the other hand, I agree that we cannot understand God.

Examiner's comments

An excellent answer on one side – that God can be understood. But Level 4 requires 'reasoned consideration of two different points of view' and the student only briefly mentions a different opinion but does not support it with reasons. Mark: 3/5

---

action point
Which of these kinds of revelation are 'general' and which are 'special'?

did you know?
The Bible is an example of special revelation, but contains examples of God revealing himself through both general and special revelation.

hints and tips
You must be able to identify *two* religious writings and *two* religious leaders from *two* religious traditions and explain how God may be known through them.

exam watch
Before you answer evaluation questions, you should plan in rough what to say for each side of the argument. It helps to write: 'On the one hand, I agree because…' and 'On the other hand, I disagree because…'

Examination practice

a Explain ways in which God is described and understood in *two* religious traditions. (6 marks) (AQA, 2002)

b Explain why religious believers have different ideas about God. (6 marks) (NEAB, 1999)

c 'Revelation by itself is enough for a person to know God.' Do you agree? Give reasons for your answer, showing that you have thought about more than one point of view. (5 marks) (NEAB, 1998)

Checklist for revision

	Understand and know	Need more revision	Do not understand
I know how God's nature is understood in Christianity and in a different religious tradition (or from a different perspective within Christianity).	☐	☐	☐
I know what a believer means by describing God as:			
• personal	☐	☐	☐
• impersonal	☐	☐	☐
• immanent	☐	☐	☐
• transcendent	☐	☐	☐
• 'One'.	☐	☐	☐
I know one difficulty or question connected with describing God in *each* of these ways.	☐	☐	☐
I know the difference between monotheism and polytheism.	☐	☐	☐
I know why some believers prefer to think of God as 'One' and others to think of God as having different 'aspects' or 'forms'.	☐	☐	☐
I know at least *three* arguments why some say God cannot be known.	☐	☐	☐
I know at least *three* arguments why others say God can be known.	☐	☐	☐
I know the difference between general and special revelation.	☐	☐	☐
I can give examples of each from *two* religious traditions.	☐	☐	☐
I understand what people can learn about God through:			
• nature	☐	☐	☐
• the lives and work of religious leaders	☐	☐	☐
• religious writings	☐	☐	☐
• worship	☐	☐	☐
• personal experience.	☐	☐	☐

SECTION B: THINKING ABOUT MORALITY

5 Ways of making moral decisions

What do I need to know?

- **Absolute morality** and examples of people who take this stance.
- **Relative morality** and examples of people who take this stance.
- **Sources of moral authority**: **conscience**, scripture, tradition, **reason**, religious leaders.
- How do people's beliefs affect their behaviour?
- Should religious beliefs affect behaviour more than other beliefs?
- Can religious people claim to hold beliefs about moral issues that they do not practise?

The difference between absolute and relative morality

An absolute moralist believes that if something is wrong, it is always wrong no matter what the circumstances. For example, many Roman Catholics believe abortion is wrong no matter what situation the mother faces. Absolute moralists keep to their principles regardless of the consequences of any actions or choices that they might make.

A relative moralist believes that something can be wrong in some circumstances but not in others. For example, some Anglican and Protestant Christians believe abortion is generally wrong, but they might feel it was acceptable for a woman to have an abortion if the pregnancy was a result of rape. They would take individual circumstances into account in each case.

Sources of moral authority

These guide people in their moral decisions. They provide the authority on which people base their actions.

Conscience

Three sources of moral authority for Christians

Religious leader   Scripture

hints and tips

In this section you must refer to *two* religious traditions, one of which must be Christianity, when you are discussing moral issues.

exam watch

You will be asked about absolute and relative morality in the context of moral issues. For example, you might be asked what someone who believes in absolute morality would say about divorce.

exam watch

You will be asked about sources of moral authority in the context of moral issues. For example, you could be asked for two sources of moral authority that would help a believer decide whether abortion was right or wrong.

25

Revise for GCSE Religious Studies AQA B: Thinking about God and morality

Conscience: an inner sense of right and wrong; a feeling of guilt when you do wrong. Some say you are born with it, or that it comes from God, or from your upbringing.

Scripture: sacred writings or holy books, for example the Vedas (Hindu) or Guru Granth Sahib (Sikh).

Tradition: the customs and beliefs handed down through generations; the religious teachings of the faith over the centuries.

Reason: the mind deciding what the consequences of an action would be.

Religious leaders: these can be the founders or great leaders of a religion like Moses (Jewish) or Siddhatta Gotama (Buddhist), or religious leaders of the present time like the Pope (Roman Catholic), or even leaders of local religious communities like the imam (Muslim) or minister (Baptist Christian).

> **exam watch**
> In every essay question, one part will always be about how beliefs affect behaviour. Make sure you think about this for each moral issue.

> **action point**
> Try to answer the last two questions in the bullet points under 'What do I need to know?' These are evaluation questions so you need to think about more than one point of view.

Short questions

a Using examples, explain the difference between absolute and relative morality. (4 marks)

b Give *two* different sources of moral authority which could help a person decide whether an action was right or wrong. (2 marks)

c **i** Name *two* different religious leaders from two religious traditions. (2 marks)
   ii Explain how a religious leader is a source of moral authority. (2 marks)

Checklist for revision

	Understand and know	Need more revision	Do not understand
I know the difference between absolute morality and relative morality.	☐	☐	☐
I know an example of each in *two* religious traditions.	☐	☐	☐
I know the meaning of:			
• conscience	☐	☐	☐
• scripture	☐	☐	☐
• tradition	☐	☐	☐
• reason.	☐	☐	☐
I can identify religious leaders in *two* religious traditions.	☐	☐	☐
I understand how religious beliefs affect moral choices.	☐	☐	☐
I understand how moral beliefs are carried out in practice.	☐	☐	☐

SECTION B: THINKING ABOUT MORALITY

6 Abortion

What do I need to know?
- Concepts of **sanctity of life** and **quality of life**.
- Reasons used by religious believers for and against abortion.
- Differing religious responses to situations when abortion is supported.
- Application of sacred texts, religious principles and statements by religious authorities to abortion.

Concepts of sanctity of life and quality of life
Most religious arguments about abortion centre on these two ideas.

- When believers talk about the sanctity of life they mean that life is a precious gift from God, therefore it is sacred (holy) and worthy of the highest respect. It is not up to us to take life away from anyone, it is up to God.
- Quality of life is about being able to experience life and communicate with others, being fulfilled and content inside yourself. If a person was being kept alive artificially or was in constant terrible pain, some would describe their quality of life as poor.

Arguments against abortion
- The foetus is a child with a soul from the first moment of conception.
- Life is sacred, given by God and only God can take it away (sanctity of life).
- The unborn baby, even a handicapped one, has the same human rights as anyone else; it should be protected.
- Every baby is unique – no one can know how valuable that child's life might be.
- Abortion can be used selfishly – as birth control or for social reasons.

Arguments in favour of abortion
- It is cruel to bring a severely handicapped baby with a poor quality of life into the world.
- It is the mother's body, therefore it is her decision.
- The mother's circumstances (for example, finances, the effect of a handicapped child on her family, whether she could care for the baby) should be considered.
- The foetus is not really a person yet, but the woman is a person (loved by friends and family).
- The risk to the mother's health outweighs the rights of the baby.
- It is a matter for an individual's conscience.

hints and tips
In this section you must refer to *two* religious traditions, one of which must be Christianity.

beware
Quality of life is *not* about having plenty of money and material possessions.

hints and tips
In general, sanctity of life is used in arguments *against* abortion, and quality of life is used in arguments *for* abortion.

Religious responses to situations when abortion is supported

Many Roman Catholics believe killing an unborn child is morally wrong under all circumstances (absolute morality). Other Christians accept abortion if the baby was going to be seriously deformed, the mother's life was in danger, or if the pregnancy was a result of rape. Baptists, Methodists and Evangelists think it is up to the individual (conscience) to decide based on the Christian principle of love. The rights of the unborn baby have to be balanced against the mother's rights, depending on the circumstances (relative morality).

Most Jews accept abortion if the mother's life is in danger. Some would also allow it if the baby's birth would lead the mother to despair or suicide. Some Reform Jews would include being poor, which might affect the mother's mental health. In Israel, abortion is legal when the mother is under sixteen, a victim of rape or incest, and when the baby would be severely mentally or physically handicapped. Most Jewish authorities think the baby becomes a person with rights at birth, so until then can be sacrificed for the sake of the mother.

Muslims oppose abortion in all cases except where the mother's life is in danger. Most would say that even a handicapped child should not be aborted. Allah has a plan for that individual. Abortion for economic reasons is forbidden.

Hindus oppose all taking of life including abortion (ahimsa – non-violence). The soul is present in every living thing. But Hinduism teaches that life begins at birth so abortion could be possible when a mother's life is at risk.

Buddhists think life begins at conception; therefore all abortion is killing and has harmful karmic effects. Some accept abortion if the baby will have a severe handicap, but they accept this will cause personal suffering and harmful consequences.

Sikhs believe life begins at conception so abortion is wrong. But if the woman had been raped, abortion might be permissible. Severe handicap is not a good enough reason to have an abortion, but Sikhs recognize the right of parents to make their own decision in such cases.

> **did you know?**
> - Abortion is legal in Britain up to 24 weeks in the pregnancy, but a woman whose life or health are at risk, or whose child will be handicapped, can have an abortion at any time.
> - For a legal abortion to take place two doctors need to agree that the mother's physical or mental health or her life is at risk, or her existing family will suffer, or the child will be born handicapped.

Religious teachings on abortion

Christianity and Judaism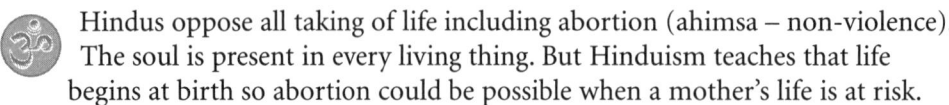

- The commandment: 'Do not commit murder.' (Exodus 20: 13)
- Special creation of human life: 'So God created human beings, making them to be like himself.' (Genesis 1: 27)
- Sanctity of life.
- 'I chose you before I gave you life, and before you were born.' (Jeremiah 1: 5) The belief that God is in the foetus from conception and has a plan for each person.

Christianity

Roman Catholic: The Didache states, 'You shall not kill by abortion the fruit of the womb and you shall not murder the infant already born.' Pope Paul VI in *Humanae Vitae* (1968) said that abortion was always wrong and that human life was sacred. 'Life must be protected with the utmost care from the moment of conception: abortion and infanticide are abominable crimes.' (*Gaudium et Spes* 51, Second Vatican Council)

The Church of England (1984) said that every human life is unique and that the foetus should be respected and protected, but its life is not absolutely paramount. Sometimes abortion is the lesser of two evils.

The Methodist Synod (1976) said that abortion might be justified if the life of the mother was in danger or the child would be severely abnormal. The woman's other children, bad housing and family poverty should also be taken into consideration.

Judaism

'If a woman in labour has a life-threatening difficulty, one dismembers the embryo within her…for her life takes precedence over its life.' (The Talmud)

Islam

'Do not kill your children in fear of poverty. We shall provide for both them and you. Killing them is a big sin.' (The Qur'an, surah 17: 31) The Qur'an says that a mother should not be treated unfairly because of her child. Yet the Hadith says, 'No severer of womb relationship ties will ever enter paradise.' Some say the foetus is 'ensouled' at 120 days so abortions before that time are not killing a living person.

Hinduism

The soul is present in every living thing: 'In Him all things exist, from Him all things originate. He has become all. He exists on every side. He is truly the all.' (Mahabharata Shanti Parva 47–56) Gandhi said ahimsa (non-violence) might permit killing if it were founded on a totally unselfish motive, in order to bring about some spiritual benefit. Many Hindus would follow advice given by their friends or priest.

Buddhism

Abortion breaks the first precept of not harming others but it might be needed for 'compassionate reasons' in particular circumstances. (General Secretary, The Buddhist Society)

Sikhism

At the time of the Gurus, baby girls were sometimes killed for economic reasons. This practice was condemned in the Rahit Maryada and the teaching is now used as a reason for protecting all forms of life. General principles: God is the creator of all; life has a purpose; sanctity of life. Guru Nanak said, 'God sends us and we take birth. God calls us back and we die.' (Adi Granth 1239)

Short questions

a Explain *two* circumstances when abortion is regarded as acceptable by believers in *one* religious tradition. (4 marks) (NEAB, 2001)

b Explain *two* circumstances when abortion is regarded as wrong by believers in a *different* religious tradition. (4 marks) (NEAB, 2001)

c Give two options other than abortion that are open to a woman who has an unwanted pregnancy. (2 marks) (NEAB, 2001)

Examination type questions

a How might Christians use the terms 'sanctity of life' and 'quality of life' in arguments about abortion? (5 marks) (AQA, 2002)

b 'It's the woman's body. She is the only person who has the right to choose whether or not to have an abortion.' Do you agree? Give reasons for your answer, showing that you have thought about more than one point of view. Refer to religious teachings in your answer. (5 marks) (AQA, 2002)

Student's answer

a *Christians might use 'sanctity of life' to argue that abortion is wrong. God has created life, therefore only God has the right to end the life of the unborn baby. Each person was made in God's image, therefore each person is holy, like God, and special. Other Christians might use 'quality of life' to argue for abortion. If the baby were severely handicapped so that it could not do anything for itself, what kind of life would that be? It would be more loving to prevent a child like that coming into the world.*

b *I agree. The woman has to care for the child and only she knows whether she will be able to cope. She might be an unmarried mother or already have too many children. She might have even been raped. No one else can judge her situation.*

Examiner's comments

a An excellent answer for sanctity of life, correctly applying it to an argument against abortion, and a good application of quality of life to an argument for abortion. Mark: 5/5

b A one-sided answer, with no reference to religious teachings. No consideration of the father's rights or the rights of the baby, nor any mention of a religious perspective. Mark: 3/5

Examination practice

'A pregnant woman has been told that she will have a severely handicapped child. She is advised to consider an abortion.'

a i Explain why believers in *one* religious tradition are against abortion in the situation outlined above. (5 marks) (NEAB, 1998)

ii Explain why believers in a *different* religious tradition think abortion may be justified in the same situation. (4 marks) (NEAB, 1998)

b State and explain *two* circumstances, other than the example above, when abortion is regarded by some religious believers as acceptable. (6 marks) (NEAB, 1998)

c 'If a baby is not wanted by its mother, there are many people who would adopt it. It should not be killed.' Do you agree? Give reasons for your answer, showing that you have thought about more than one point of view. (5 marks) (NEAB, 1998)

Checklist for revision

	Understand and know	Need more revision	Do not understand
I know the meaning of sanctity of life and quality of life.	☐	☐	☐
I know how these terms are used in arguments for and against abortion.	☐	☐	☐
I know the reasons used by believers in *two* religious traditions in favour of abortion.	☐	☐	☐
I know the reasons used by believers in *two* religious traditions against abortion.	☐	☐	☐
I can apply these reasons to different situations, for example, rape, risk to mother, and so on.	☐	☐	☐
I know *two* quotations from sacred texts, religious principles or statements by religious authorities from each of *two* religious traditions.	☐	☐	☐

SECTION B: THINKING ABOUT MORALITY

7 Sex, marriage and divorce

What do I need to know?

- Religious attitudes to sex before and outside marriage.
- Reasons for contrasting religious views towards contraception and divorce.
- Religious understandings of the purpose and character of marriage.
- Religious responses to the issues of love, parental involvement and race in the choice of marriage partner.
- Application of sacred texts, religious principles and statements by religious authorities to sex, marriage and divorce.
- Concepts of **commitment**, responsibility, **contract** and **covenant**.

hints and tips
In this section you must refer to *two* religious traditions, one of which must be Christianity.

Religious attitudes to sex before marriage

 Christianity teaches that sex before marriage is wrong for the following reasons.

- Sex belongs within marriage; it is the expression of a deep, loving, life-long union between a couple.
- Sex is a gift of God demanding responsibility, commitment and total love.
- It is wrong to use people as sex objects.
- Chastity is important. For example, 'True Love Waits' pledges not to have sex before marriage.
- Sex can create new life (one of its main purposes – Roman Catholic teaching).
- St Paul urged sexual restraint and control: 'You know that your bodies are parts of the body of Christ'; 'Avoid immorality…the man who is guilty of sexual immorality sins against his own body. Don't you know that your body is the temple of the Holy Spirit, who lives in you and who was given to you by God?' (1 Corinthians 6: 15, 18–19)
- It would be irresponsible for a Christian to risk pregnancy or spread sexually transmitted diseases.

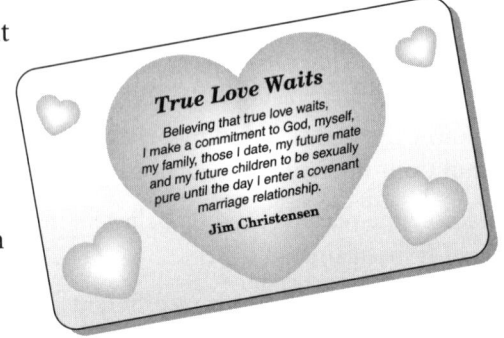

A promise made by a Christian teenager

No religion is in favour of sex before marriage. It is forbidden in Judaism and Sikhism, and expressly forbidden in the Qur'an (Islam) and in Hindu scriptures and society. Buddhists warn that sex before marriage is a cause of suffering because it is based on the desire for pleasure rather than love, so should be avoided.

Religious attitudes to sex outside marriage (adultery)

 Christianity teaches that adultery is wrong for the following reasons.

- It breaks the promises (vows) people make when they marry.

32

7 Sex, marriage and divorce

- It is against the commandment: 'Do not commit adultery.' (Exodus 20: 14)
- It is against Jesus' teaching: 'You have heard that it was said, "Do not commit adultery." But now I tell you: anyone who looks at a woman and wants to possess her has already committed adultery with her in his heart.' (Matthew 5: 27–8). The woman caught in adultery was forgiven but her sin was condemned (John 8: 1–11).
- It usually involves deception, breaking trust – honesty is essential to marriage.
- It threatens the stable relationship needed for children's security.
- Roman Catholics view sex as a sacramental sign of Christ's love for the Church. Extra-marital sex cannot be that sign.
- It is against the purpose of marriage.

No religion is in favour of sex outside marriage (adultery).

Buddhism

Buddhists avoid sexual misconduct, which causes unhappiness to others. Buddha taught that once married, a man should look upon other women as his mother, sister or daughter, so even the thought of adultery is harmful. 'Four things happen to the thoughtless man who takes another man's wife: he lowers himself, his pleasure is restless, he is blamed by others, he goes to hell.' (Dhammapada 309)

Judaism

'Do not commit adultery.' (Exodus 20: 14)

Hinduism

Adultery is disapproved of; chastity is important.

Islam

'Have nothing to do with adultery, for it is a shameful thing, and an evil opening the way to other evils.' (The Qur'an, surah 17: 32)

Sikhism

'Do not cast your eyes on the beauty of another's wife.' (Adi Granth 274) 'A Sikh should respect another man's wife as he would his own mother.' (Rahit Maryada)

Religious views towards contraception and divorce

Contraception

Christian views on contraception vary. All Christians believe in 'responsible parenthood'; children should be wanted and welcomed. The Orthodox and Roman Catholic Churches teach that the use of artificial contraception within marriage is wrong (absolute morality). The Roman Catholic teaching is based on the following reasons.

- Contraception goes against one purpose of marriage, to have a family.
- Using artificial contraception might encourage infidelity.

- Artificial contraception is against natural law, but the rhythm method is acceptable.
- Every sexual act should have the possibility of creating new life, according to the Pope. (*Humanae Vitae*, 1968)

Most Christian churches allow contraception if both partners agree to use it. The method is up to them. Their reasons include the following.

- If couples wait, they will have more money, so children will be wanted and have the proper care and attention they need.
- Methodists accept contraception for 'spacing' children so the mother's health is not harmed by too many pregnancies and for helping the couple to develop their relationship more fully before such a commitment.
- In an overcrowded, poverty ridden world, it would be unfair to bring a child into a life of deprivation.

Divorce

All Christians agree that, ideally, marriage is for life. Jesus taught that no one must separate what God had joined together and that anyone who divorced and re-married was committing adultery (Mark 10: 1–12). The Church must keep marriage sacred but needs to love and care for those who are divorced.

- Roman Catholics see marriage as a sacrament that cannot be undone until death parts the couple. The couple cannot re-marry. Annulment is the only possibility (absolute morality).
- The Church of England now allows divorced couples to re-marry in church with the bishop's permission.
- The Eastern Orthodox Church itself grants divorces and re-marries couples, but usually not more than twice.
- Protestant churches accept civil divorce and allow re-marriage in church.

The Bible says a man can divorce his wife if she is guilty of some shameful conduct (Deuteronomy 24: 1). Jews think of marriage as a voluntary contract, so allow divorce (a get) if both people agree to it, but only as a last resort. The couple must try reconciliation first, but if they no longer love each other as 'one flesh', they can part. Jews think divorce is sad but not a disgrace and people are encouraged to re-marry.

Muslims think of marriage as a contract so divorce is allowed as a last resort but is hateful to Allah (Hadith). The couple must wait three months (iddah) to see if the wife is pregnant and to allow reconciliation if possible. 'If you fear a breach between a man and his wife, appoint two arbiters, one from his family and the other from hers. If both want to be brought back together, Allah will settle things between them.' (The Qur'an, surah 4: 35) The man must return any dowry and must provide for her until she re-marries. A wife can divorce her husband, but if it is not his fault, he does not have to support her and she must repay the marriage gift (mahr). He still has responsibility for his children's support in all cases.

 Hindu scriptures teach that marriage should be for life. It is a normal stage of life and an important way of handing down values. Divorce is allowed in

---

hints and tips

Most other religions allow contraception if it is used by mutual consent and not to avoid having children altogether.

Muslims would agree with this but would oppose any method that caused an abortion. Some Muslims think contraception is wrong, that it interferes with Allah's plans, and that Allah gives people the strength to cope with any children.

Orthodox Judaism only allows the use of contaception when pregnancy risks the mother's health and not for social or economic reasons. However, Orthodox Judaism does not allow the use of condoms or the rhythm method, which wastes semen.

7 Sex, marriage and divorce

India if the husband is cruel or the couple cannot have children after fifteen years of marriage. A law of Manu says that a wife must respect even an unfaithful husband. People can re-marry legally but it is rare because of the social stigma attached to divorce.

See also teaching on adultery, pages 32–33.

 A couple should stay faithful and married for life. The things that lead to unhappy marriages, like intolerance and lack of trust, also stop spiritual growth. Divorce will bring harmful consequences, but some marriages fail and therefore divorce should go ahead sensitively to limit the harm done.

Marriage should be for life – the couple should be 'one spirit in two bodies' (Guru Amar Das). Divorce is reluctantly accepted. The family's pride is hurt and they try to do everything possible to prevent the separation. Sikhs can re-marry in the presence of the Guru Granth Sahib.

The purpose and character of marriage

Christian wedding vows describe the purpose and character of marriage.

Purpose

- Love: companionship through good times and bad.
- Sex: to control and direct the sexual instinct.
- Children: to have children and bring them up according to God's will.

Character

- Faithfulness: sexual fidelity.
- 'Until death do us part': a lifetime's commitment before God.
- A spiritual bond: a chance to develop trust, faithfulness, mutual consideration, reverence and love.
- A contract or covenant with particular responsibilities to love, care for, and be faithful towards one's partner, and to bring up children in a secure, loving way.

Other religions also think marriage should be for companionship, for a proper sexual relationship, for opportunities to develop spiritual qualities, and it should have faithfulness in commitment.

Love, parental involvement and race in the choice of marriage partner

Christians believe that love is essential to marriage. Parents are not usually involved in the choice of partner but would hope that their child would marry someone who shares their Christian values. However, some Christians living in traditional societies have arranged marriages. There is no objection to race. Christians believe in equality.

 Some Orthodox communities have arranged marriages by parents; others practise free choice. Race is not a problem, except that it is important Jews marry Jewish partners so that the children are considered Jewish.

 Parents usually arrange marriages. They look for someone who would be

Revise for GCSE Religious Studies AQA B: Thinking about God and morality

personally compatible, from a similar social background, and sharing sound religious beliefs and values. Islam views all races as equals and religious values are more important than race.

In India, family elders usually arrange marriages, sometimes consulting horoscopes to confirm the person is suitable. If young people choose their own partners, the parents only approve if the families are socially equal. In Britain, parents may arrange introductions, but now many young Hindus choose their own partners. Race is not as important as caste (social position).

In traditional Buddhist countries parents arrange marriages. In Britain, Buddhists choose their own partners. Mixed race marriages are accepted.

In Britain, young Sikhs have a say in their choice of partner, but parents and other relatives still like to be involved. Marriages based on love are not entirely trusted, although arranged marriages are not really in keeping with Sikh ethics. In rural Punjab, extended families may choose marriage partners. Sikh scripture says that caste or birth should not matter. There are no problems about mixed race marriages, as Sikhs believe in equality. However, a Sikh's daughter must marry a Sikh.

Short questions

a **i** How are parents involved in the choice of their children's marriage partners in *two* religious traditions? (4 marks) (NEAB, 1998)

  ii What attitudes are taken by these traditions towards mixed race marriages? (4 marks) (NEAB, 1998)

b Besides bringing up children, give *two* other purposes of marriage according to a religious tradition. (4 marks) (NEAB, 1997)

c Explain how a Christian marriage relationship is a 'covenant'. (2 marks) (NEAB, 2000)

d Give *three* reasons why a Christian would regard adultery as wrong. (3 marks) (NEAB, 2000)

Examination type questions

a **i** Choose *one* religious tradition which teaches that using artificial contraception within marriage is wrong. Explain why they think it is wrong. (4 marks) (NEAB, 2001)

  ii Choose a *different* religious tradition which teaches that using artificial contraception within marriage is acceptable. Explain why they think it is acceptable. (4 marks) (NEAB, 2001)

Student's answer

a **i** Roman Catholics think using contraception is wrong because they think every time you have sex you should have a baby. It is going against God's plan as it is up to God to decide how many children you should have.

  ii Other Christians disagree. They think it is all right to use contraception to plan your family so that you have enough money to bring up a child. A couple might not be ready to have a family as soon as they get married. Also, having too many children could mean they do not all get the attention they need.

7 Sex, marriage and divorce

Examiner's comments

a i The candidate gives two reasons for the Roman Catholic attitude: sex should be open to the possibility of creating new life and contraception interferes with God's plan. However, it is not true that 'every time you have sex you should have a baby'! No mention is made of the purpose of marriage or papal teaching in *Humanae Vitae*, or the idea that contraception might encourage infidelity.
Mark: 2/4

ii Two main points are made: having enough money to support a child and proper care for children. However, there is no religious reason given, for example the Methodist teaching that couples need to strengthen their own relationship before making the commitment to a family. This would have brought the answer up to Level 3.
Mark: 2/4

Examination practice

a Explain different attitudes towards divorce in *two* religious traditions. (8 marks) (NEAB, 1999)

b How might *one* of these religions help couples who are having problems in their marriage? (3 marks) (NEAB, 1999)

c 'Couples who are having problems should stay together for the sake of the children.' Do you agree? Give reasons for your answer, showing that you have thought about more than one point of view. (5 marks) (NEAB, 1999)

Checklist for revision

	Understand and know	Need more revision	Do not understand
I know *two* religious attitudes towards sex before marriage.	☐	☐	☐
I know *two* religious attitudes towards sex outside of marriage (adultery).	☐	☐	☐
I understand what marriage is for (purpose) in *two* religions.	☐	☐	☐
I understand what marriage should be like (character) in *two* religions.	☐	☐	☐
I know *two* religious views about love, parental involvement and race when it comes to choosing a marriage partner.	☐	☐	☐
I know at least *two* religious texts, principles or statements by religious authorities on sex, marriage and divorce.	☐	☐	☐
I know the meaning of:			
• commitment	☐	☐	☐
• responsibility	☐	☐	☐
• contract	☐	☐	☐
• covenant.	☐	☐	☐

SECTION B: THINKING ABOUT MORALITY

8 Prejudice and discrimination

What do I need to know?

- Causes of **prejudice** and **discrimination**.
- At least two different forms of prejudice and discrimination.
- Religious attitudes to prejudice and discrimination.
- Application of sacred texts, religious principles and statements by religious authorities to prejudice and discrimination.
- Concepts of **equality**, **justice** and **community**.

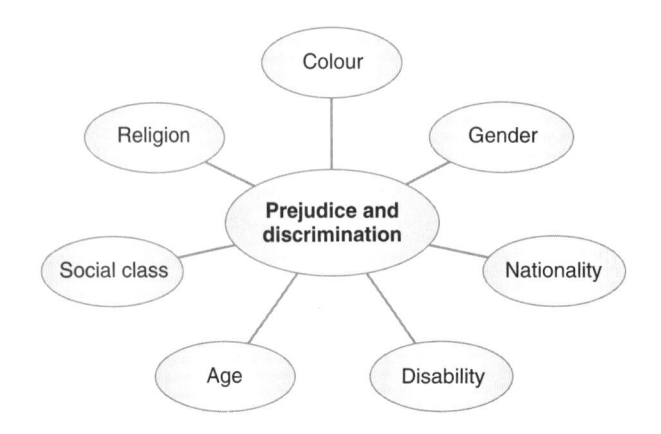

hints and tips

In this section you must refer to *two* religious traditions, one of which must be Christianity.

Prejudice literally means to pre-judge someone, to have an opinion about them based not on facts but on stereotyped assumptions about them; for example, thinking that all teenagers browsing in stores are probably shoplifters.

Discrimination means acting on a prejudice, treating someone unfairly or stopping them from doing something because of prejudice; for example, refusing to give someone a job because they are black.

The main causes of prejudice and discrimination are:

- ignorance
- upbringing
- fear
- stereotyping.

Different forms of prejudice and discrimination

Forms of prejudice and discrimination

action point

Try to think of *two* ways people might be discriminated against in each of these cases. For example:

Religion: In the past, Roman Catholics in Northern Ireland could not get certain jobs, for example, in the police force. Jews were put to death in concentration camps by the Nazis.

Concepts of equality, justice and community

Most religions teach about the basic equality of all human beings. This does not mean everyone is the same or even that everyone has equal advantages in life – they obviously do not. 'Everyone is equal' means that all people have equal human rights to live and work freely and to search for happiness and peace.

Religious believers think people should be treated with justice – fairly and according to the law. If laws are unjust, they work to change them.

Many religious believers have an important sense of community, people who share the same values and feel responsible for each other.

Religious attitudes to prejudice and discrimination

Christianity

- Everyone is created by God and equal in God's sight.
- 'Love your neighbour as you love yourself.' (Matthew 22: 39)
- 'From one human being he created all races on earth and made them live throughout the whole earth.' (Acts 17: 26)
- Jesus' teaching: The Good Samaritan (Luke 10: 25–37); The Centurion's Servant (Luke 7: 1–10).
- Jesus' example: helping the disabled and treatment of those of different religious beliefs (for example, the Samaritan woman). The kingdom of God was open to everyone. In fact, poor and outcast people were more likely to get into the kingdom first.
- St Paul's teaching: 'There is no longer any distinction between Gentiles and Jews…Christ is all, Christ is in all.' (Colossians 3: 11)
- Discrimination on grounds of sex, race, colour, social conditions, language or religion is incompatible with God's design. (*The Church in the Modern World*, Second Vatican Council)

Judaism

- Everyone is created by God and equal in God's sight.
- 'Love your neighbour as you love yourself.' (Leviticus 19: 18)
- The Torah teaches that foreigners should be treated with compassion, just like the poor; part of the crops should be left for them (Leviticus 19: 9–10). 'Do not deprive foreigners and orphans of their rights.' (Deuteronomy 24: 17)
- Prophets like Amos and Isaiah taught that social justice was more pleasing to God than religious ceremonies.
- The story of Jonah's attitude to Nineveh shows God's disapproval of prejudice and narrow racism.
- Jews attach great importance to the role of the mother in bringing their children up in the religion. They regard men and women as equals but having different obligations.

> **action point**
> The idea of community is central to many faiths. Find out about *two* of these ideas: the ummah (Islam), the sangha (Buddhism), the Body of Christ (Christianity), synagogue (Judaism), Sadhsangat and Khalsa (Sikhism).

> **did you know?**
> In Britain, racial discrimination is against the law under the Race Relations Act 1976 and gender discrimination is illegal under the Sex Discrimination Act 1975.

> **action point**
> Find out what role women play in *two* religious traditions. Are they treated as equals?

- Experience of the Holocaust makes them particularly aware of the evils of prejudice and discrimination.

Islam

- Allah created all people equal: 'O mankind, We created you from a single pair of a male and a female, and made you into tribes and nations that you may know each other (not that you despise each other).' (The Qur'an, surah 49: 13) Equality is also emphasized in the Hajj.

- God's power is shown in the variety of his creations: 'And among His Signs is the creation of the heavens and the earth, and the variations in your languages and your colours.' (The Qur'an, surah 30: 22)

- Muhammad taught that differences in colour, tribe, race or traditions are not to be used as excuses for unjust treatment. He preached against slavery, angering the Makkans.

- All people are considered Muslims and when they turn to Islam in later life, Muslims call them 'reverts' – reverting back to their true faith.

- Islamic law is founded on the spirit of justice: 'Allah does not look upon your outward appearance; He looks upon your hearts and your deeds.' (Hadith)

Hinduism

- Hindus have a duty to regard all with respect no matter who they are because they have been created by God.

- 'I look upon all creatures equally; none are less dear to me and none more dear. But those who worship me with love, live in me and I come to life in them.' (Bhagavad Gita 9: 29)

- Regarding women: 'Where women are honoured, there the gods shower blessings; but where they are ill-treated, sacred rites bring no rewards.' (the laws of Manu 5: 55–6)

- Men and women of any caste have potential for spiritual achievement. In the Bhagavad Gita 9: 32, Krishna says, 'By taking refuge in me, O Arjuna, women, merchants (vaishya) and artisans (shudra), though lowly born (and having a low social status), also reach the highest goal' (that is, attain moksha or release).

- However, Hindu teaching about varna ('colour' literally, but meaning caste or position in society) does involve discrimination.

Buddhism

- Right action and loving kindness (metta) are central to Buddhism.

- The Buddha taught that all members of the sangha were equal and he gave full ordination to women, although reluctantly.

- When enlightenment is reached there is no more division between male and female.

- Tibetan Buddhist prayer: 'May all beings have happiness...and live believing in the equality of all that lives.'

- His Holiness the Dalai Lama has said, 'We must build a closer relationship among ourselves, based on mutual trust, mutual understanding, mutual respect, and mutual help, irrespective of culture, philosophy, religion or faith.'

Sikhism

- Equality is emphasized in the gurdwara – all sit on the floor, women take part.
- 'All men and women are equal – all are children of God.' (Adi Granth 611)
- All people are worshipping the same God no matter what religion they follow and Sikhism has always been tolerant of other faiths for this reason.
- One God is the source of all life. God has no colour or form. To discriminate on grounds of race, religion or gender is wrong according to Sikh belief.
- 'Know people by the light which illumines them, not by their caste. In the hereafter no one is regarded as different from another on grounds of caste.' (Adi Granth 349)
- Guru Nanak criticized the idea of being an 'untouchable': 'All impurity contracted by touch is mere superstition.' (Adi Granth 472)

> **hints and tips**
> You should also find out how some religious believers have fought against various forms of prejudice and discrimination or how they might try to do so now.

Short questions

a Using examples, explain the difference between prejudice and discrimination. (4 marks) (NEAB, 1997)

b Give *two* reasons why some people are prejudiced. (2 marks) (NEAB, 2000)

c Describe *three* ways in which religious believers could fight prejudice and discrimination. (6 marks) (AQA, 2002)

Examination type questions

a Explain how and why people may be discriminated against because of *one* of these things: race, gender, social class, religion, physical handicap. (4 marks) (NEAB, 2001)

b Give *two* ways in which a religious believer could help in the situation you have described. (2 marks) (NEAB, 2001)

Student's answer

a People can be discriminated against because of their race by not being given a job if they are black. More black people are out of work than white. Black people are called names and have racist jokes made about them. My friend is black and he is always getting stopped by the police for no reason.

b A religious believer could help by refusing to listen to racist jokes and by employing more black people (if they are the boss).

Examiner's comments

a The candidate describes *how* people can be discriminated against because of race in terms of jobs, personal abuse and harassment, but does not say *why* these occur. However, a range of ways was given.
Mark: 3/4

b Two simple ways were given.
Mark: 2/2

Examination practice

a Choose *two* different religious traditions and outline the teachings of each about prejudice and discrimination. (8 marks) (NEAB, 1998)

b How do people in *one* religious tradition put these teachings into practise? (4 marks) (NEAB, 1998)

c 'By sending their children to religious schools, some religious believers are encouraging them to be prejudiced against others.' Do you agree? Give reasons for your answer, showing that you have thought about more than one point of view. (5 marks) (NEAB, 1998)

Checklist for revision

	Understand and know	Need more revision	Do not understand
I know the difference between prejudice and discrimination.	☐	☐	☐
I can give an example of each.	☐	☐	☐
I know *three* causes of prejudice and discrimination.	☐	☐	☐
I know about *two* of these forms of prejudice and discrimination in detail:			
• colour/race	☐	☐	☐
• gender	☐	☐	☐
• religion	☐	☐	☐
• age	☐	☐	☐
• class	☐	☐	☐
• disability	☐	☐	☐
• nationality.	☐	☐	☐
I know what *two* religions teach about prejudice and discrimination.	☐	☐	☐
I know *two* sacred texts or statements by religious authorities about prejudice and discrimination, or equality in general, from *two* religions.	☐	☐	☐
I can explain how the teachings are put into practise.	☐	☐	☐
I understand the meaning of:			
• equality	☐	☐	☐
• justice	☐	☐	☐
• community.	☐	☐	☐
I understand how these ideas are important in discussions about prejudice and discrimination.	☐	☐	☐

SECTION B: THINKING ABOUT MORALITY

9 World poverty

What do I need to know?

- Reasons used by religious believers for caring for the poor.
- Ways in which religious believers care for those in need.
- The work of a religious organization that helps to alleviate world poverty.
- Application of sacred texts, religious principles and statements by religious authorities to world poverty.
- Concepts of justice, **stewardship** and compassion.

hints and tips

In this section you must refer to *two* religious traditions, one of which must be Christianity.

Concepts of justice, stewardship and compassion

Poverty is a vicious circle. The poor lack education, work, health care, housing, food and water. They fall victim to disease, drought and debt. Religious believers think people should be treated fairly (with justice) (see pages 38–39). Yet many would say that world poverty is made worse by unfair trade rules and high interest rates charged by Western banks that lead to huge debt.

The Bible teaches that God placed humans in charge of the created world to look after it on God's behalf. Humans must rule it fairly and be generous to all God's creatures. This is called stewardship.

Muslims have a similar idea: 'khalifah' or trusteeship.

Compassion means 'suffering with' someone. If people really understood the suffering of the poor, they would feel they must help them.

Why religious believers should help the poor

Christianity

- Christians must 'Love your neighbour as you love yourself' (Matthew 22: 39). Sharing is the practical way to love others.
- Old Testament teaching: 'Share your food with the hungry and open your homes to the homeless poor. Give clothes to those who have nothing to wear, and do not refuse to help your own relatives.' (Isaiah 58: 7)
- New Testament teaching: The Rich Young Man asks: 'Good teacher, what must I do to receive eternal life?'...And Jesus said, 'Go and sell all you have and give the money to the poor, and you will have riches in heaven.' (Mark 10: 17–21); the Sheep and the Goats – people will be judged on whether they have helped the neediest people (Matthew 25: 31–46); the Rich Man and Lazarus (Luke 16: 19–31); the Good Samaritan (Luke 10: 30–7).
- Jesus' example: healing miracles, feeding of the 5,000, his association with outcasts, the poor, and sinners.
- General principles: God made everyone, we are all brothers and sisters and should therefore help each other; good stewardship in Jesus' parables means wisely using wealth compassionately.

did you know?

Early Christians sold their property and distributed it among themselves so that no one was in need. See Acts 2: 45, James 2: 1–17 and 1 John 3: 17–18.

43

- Churches teach followers to give to charities and to work for justice for the poor.
- Religious leaders' example: Desmond Tutu, Mother Teresa, and Martin Luther King.

Judaism

- 'Open your hand to the poor and your neighbours in your land who are in need.' (the Jewish Bible, Deuteronomy 15: 11)
- The Bible describes responsibility for the poor:
  - sharing food the land produces, helping slaves or people in debt to make a better life for themselves, leaving land unused every seventh year for the benefit of the poor (Exodus 23: 11).
  - not fully reaping crops to leave some for the poor and foreigners (Leviticus 19: 9, 10).
- Prophets condemned those who did not share wealth with the poor. Rabbis taught charity is 'zedakah' meaning 'justice' – a duty God requires. Maimonides lists eight ways of giving in 'Jewish Values'. Ideally, charity should be given anonymously and sensitively in a way that allows the poor to keep their self-respect and to help themselves.

Islam

- 'He is not a believer who eats his fill while his neighbour remains hungry by his side.' (Hadith)
- Muslims have a duty to help the poor. The third pillar (zakah) is a way of worshipping Allah.
- All humans are equal and are special creations of Allah.
- All wealth belongs to Allah.
- Muslims are stewards of God's gifts and should use wealth to help others. Fasting during Ramadan teaches compassion for the poor.
- Poverty is a result of selfishness and greed so Muslims try to help the poor through working for justice.

Hinduism

- Hindus try to develop qualities of generosity and compassion.
- One of five daily duties is to shelter guests and Hindus may take people into their homes but also give money to the poor to fulfil this duty.
- The law of karma requires Hindus to help others who suffer. This will ensure a good rebirth and release (moksha).
- They have a tradition of generosity to members of their extended family and village.

Buddhism

- Buddhists believe greed causes suffering; wealth does not bring happiness.
- Detachment from material things is a spiritual goal, but if someone is too poor they worry and suffer. A middle way between poverty and wealth is best.
- Buddhists try to develop compassion (karuna) through meditation and by offering gifts (dana), especially food to the monks, to become unselfish.

Sikhism

- Vand chhakna (to share with others or give in charity) is a duty for Sikhs.
- The principle of Sewa (selfless service) should be practised in all areas of life.
- Guru Nanak taught: 'Only he who earns a living by the sweat of his brow and shares his earnings with others has discovered the path of righteousness' (Adi Granth 1245) and 'Be grateful to God whose bounties you enjoy; be compassionate to the needy and the people you employ.' (Guru Nanak, *Moral Issues in Six Religions* (1991)
- Sikhs believe in equality: 'He who gathers wealth by oppressing others is cursed by them.' (Guru Arjan) Sikhs are taught to recognise all humanity as one. (Guru Gobind Singh)

Ways in which religious believers care for those in need

- emergency aid
- long-term aid
- setting up or supporting charitable organizations
- personally helping or sending others to help
- prayer
- raising awareness.

The work of religious organizations

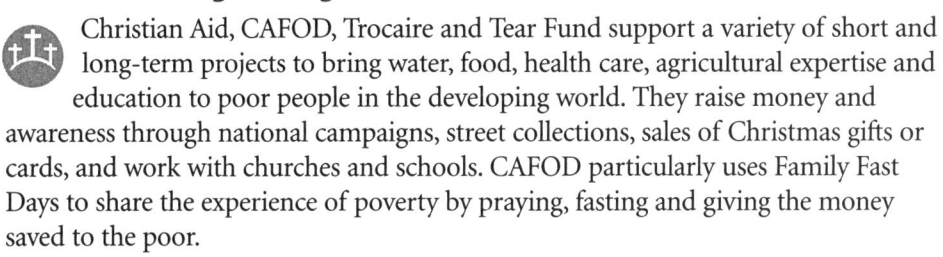

Christian Aid, CAFOD, Trocaire and Tear Fund support a variety of short and long-term projects to bring water, food, health care, agricultural expertise and education to poor people in the developing world. They raise money and awareness through national campaigns, street collections, sales of Christmas gifts or cards, and work with churches and schools. CAFOD particularly uses Family Fast Days to share the experience of poverty by praying, fasting and giving the money saved to the poor.

Tzedek is an overseas development and educational charity working in some of the poorest countries in Africa, Asia and Latin America. Tzedek is motivated by Jewish values but works beyond the Jewish community to relieve poverty regardless of religion or race.

Muslim Aid, set up in London in 1985, provides disaster relief and emergency aid, but also supports long-term projects in education, skills training, credit and agricultural schemes, water and health care.

hints and tips

You must learn what *one* religious organization does for world poverty in detail. Many have websites where you can find out about projects they are running (see below for information on the work of religious organizations).

beware

Do not use the Red Cross, Oxfam, Save the Children or any other non-religious charity.

Local temples in the UK do much to support projects and appeals. Specific organizations include ISKCON, which provides spiritual education and the world's largest vegetarian food relief programme, Orissa Appeal and Swaminarayan Organization.

Friends of the Western Buddhist Order operate the Karuna Trust, promoting education, health, skills training and cultural activities amongst some of India's poorest communities. Karuna is an ancient Buddhist word meaning 'compassionate action based on wisdom'.

Khalsa Aid is a British Sikh organization that supplies emergency disaster relief. Sikhs must give at least a tenth of their income to religious and charitable work. They donate money or other things such as goods, services or time to the gurdwara, where food is available to all, and to caring organizations.

For more information on the work of these religious organizations visit www.heinemann.co.uk/hotlinks and click on this section.

ISKCON

THE *karuna* TRUST

KHALSA AID
Recognise all of humanity as one

Short questions

a Give *two* sources of moral authority which might encourage religious believers to care for the poor.
(2 marks) (AQA, 2002)

b Explain the meaning of 'justice', 'stewardship' and 'compassion'. (3 marks)

c Explain *two* religious reasons for helping the poor from each of *two* religions. (4 marks)

Examination type questions

a Choose *one* religious tradition. Outline the work of *one* organization in this tradition that helps the poor. (4 marks) (NEAB, 2000)

b Why do believers in this tradition feel that they have a duty to help the poor? Use teachings from sacred texts or statements by religious authorities in your answer. (4 marks) (NEAB, 2000)

Student's answer

a Islam. Muslim Aid started in 1985 to bring emergency aid and relief to people in countries where natural disasters had taken place. They helped people in Bangladesh with food, houses and pumps to get clean water when floods destroyed many homes and disease was spreading. Now Muslim Aid also gives money to long-term projects in health care, education and training. They run orphanages in several countries. They try to make the people self-sufficient.

b Muslims have a duty to help the poor because they believe Allah created everyone for a purpose. Everyone's life is equally valuable to Allah, so when people suffer, they should be helped. They think wealth really belongs to Allah not us, but he made us stewards so we should use his gifts to help the poorest people.

Examiner's comments

a An excellent answer, which does not talk about the origins of the organization but gives precise details of its work, describing both emergency aid and long-term aid. Mark: 4/4

b A good answer with a range of beliefs. Allah's purpose in creation, equality, stewardship. However, there was no clear reference to sacred texts or statements by religious authorities. If the quotation, 'He is not a believer who eats his fill while his neighbour remains hungry by his side' was used, it would have reached the top level. Mark: 3/4

Examination practice

a Outline the teachings of *one* religious tradition about why believers should help the poor.
(4 marks) (NEAB, 1999)

b Describe *two* ways in which members of this tradition help poor people in developing countries.
(4 marks) (NEAB, 1999)

c 'We should look after our own people rather than those in other countries.' Do you agree? Give reasons for your answer, showing that you have thought about more than one point of view.
(5 marks) (NEAB, 1999)

Checklist for revision

	Understand and know	Need more revision	Do not understand
I know *two* reasons used by religious believers for caring for the poor.	☐	☐	☐
I can list and explain at least *three* ways believers care for the poor.	☐	☐	☐
I know at least *four* facts about the work of a religious organization that tries to help the poor in the developing world.	☐	☐	☐
I can quote *two* sacred texts or statements by a religious authority about helping to stop world poverty.	☐	☐	☐
I know the meaning of the terms:			
• justice	☐	☐	☐
• stewardship	☐	☐	☐
• compassion.	☐	☐	☐
I can apply these terms to arguments about helping the poor.	☐	☐	☐

SECTION B: THINKING ABOUT MORALITY

10 War and peace

What do I need to know?
- Reasons used by religious believers for **pacifism**.
- Reasons used by religious believers for taking part in war.
- The work of a religious believer who has worked for peace or led non-violent protest.
- Criteria for a **just war** and a **holy war** and application of each term to a relevant example.
- Application of sacred texts, religious principles and statements by religious authorities to war and peace.
- Concepts of peace, justice, and sanctity of life.

hints and tips
In this section you must refer to *two* religious traditions, one of which must be Christianity.

Pacifism is the belief that all violence is wrong no matter what the circumstances (absolute morality). Pacifists refuse to fight in wars. They are 'conscientious objectors' – they say that going to war is against their conscience.

Reasons used by religious believers for pacifism
- Violence leads to more violence.
- War solves nothing in the long run; people still have to negotiate to settle disputes.
- Gaining freedom by evil means is doing to the oppressor what the oppressed objected to in the first place.
- War wastes precious human and natural resources.
- War causes terrible suffering, even among innocent people.
- War increases hatred, prejudice and greed.

did you know?
Buddhists and Quakers (the Society of Friends) have strong traditions of pacifism.

Reasons used by religious believers for taking part in war
- These mainly centre on the idea of justice and the criteria for a just war.
- It is wrong to allow weaker countries to be attacked and do nothing about it.
- Belief in the sanctity of life requires defending the lives of the innocent.
- Self-defence is justifiable.
- In the face of great injustice, war is the lesser of two evils.
- Relative morality: it depends on the circumstances of the war.

Religious believers who have worked for peace or led non-violent protest

Martin Luther King
- led civil rights demonstrations including a march in Washington D.C. where he made the 'I have a dream' speech

hints and tips
You need to concentrate on the *work* of the person, *not* their life story.

- organized non-violent protests including sit-ins in white-only restaurants, refusing to move until served
- organized a bus boycott until blacks were allowed to sit in any seat
- gave sermons and speeches
- won the Nobel Peace Prize
- worked towards getting blacks the right to vote, to use public facilities, and to be educated with whites
- went to prison for his beliefs
- spoke out despite death threats and having his house bombed
- was finally assassinated for opposing the segregation laws in the southern USA.

Mohandas K Gandhi (also called 'Mahatma' or 'great soul')

- began non-violent 'passive resistance' or 'satyagraha' (steadfastness in truth) during twenty years of living in South Africa under apartheid
- would disregard unjust laws without hating whites or retaliating against them
- faced the consequences of his resistance
- went back to India and found the same prejudice and discrimination there between British and Indian people
- as leader of the Indian National Congress, called for the Indian people to resist British rule and gain independence by non-violent means
- led protest marches including the salt march against the salt tax
- boycotted British goods
- was repeatedly imprisoned by the British
- fasted when Indians started fighting among themselves (was prepared to die)
- campaigned to raise the status of 'untouchables' (lowest caste)
- was finally assassinated.

Just war

A just war is a war fought for a just cause.

A just war must be:

- started and controlled by a proper legal authority
- fought for a just cause (those attacked must deserve it)

> **beware**
> Jesus was *not* a pacifist. The intention of the syllabus here is to examine the work of someone in more recent history like Martin Luther King or Gandhi.

- fought to promote good or avoid evil; justice and peace must be restored afterwards
- the last resort (other ways of solving the problem tried first)
- fought using only enough force to achieve victory and innocent civilians must not be killed (proportionality)
- fought with a reasonable chance of success; the good gained by winning should outweigh the evil which led to the war.

An obligatory war (Milchemet Mitzvah) is only justifiable if it is in self-defence, that is, the enemy has attacked first or you need to strike before the enemy attacks. War must be a last resort, civilians must not be deliberately killed and care must be taken to limit the damage done to the environment. The Maimonides Code stated that when siege was laid to a city, a chance for escape should be provided. Michelmet Reshut (optional war) has not been permitted for 2,000 years.

Sometimes 'jihad' or collective defence of the Muslim community must be fought to defend the right of Muslims to follow their religion or to protect them from a tyrant. Those killed in jihad enter paradise on Judgement Day. A war is just if it has been declared by a proper authority, is a last resort, and innocent civilian life, plants and animals have been protected. The Qur'an forbids going to war to attack others, to win new land or power, or to make converts to Islam.

War must have a just cause (for example, if attacked, if power is seized illegally, exploitation of people). The Kshatriya (warrior caste) existed to defend people against oppression. Wars should be controlled and not cause unnecessary suffering. It would be unjust to kill those who surrender or are unarmed civilians, and certain weapons should not be used.

No war is just in Buddhism. Compassion for all life makes war unacceptable.

In Sikhism, a war is just (dharam yudh) if it is a last resort, a righteous cause without desire for revenge, if minimum necessary force is used, if it is fought by disciplined soldiers without the use of mercenaries, and if enemy property is respected and not taken.

Holy war

A holy war is a war fought for religious reasons 'with God on your side'.

The Crusades (Christian wars to recover Jerusalem and the holy places of Palestine from the Muslims (Turks) in the Middle Ages) were at the time considered a holy war or war on behalf of God.

In the Bible there are examples of God ordering a war or approving of war:

- 1 Samuel 15: 2–3: 'He is going to punish the people of Amalek because their ancestors opposed the Israelites…Go and attack the Amalekites and completely destroy everything they have.'
- Battle of Jericho: '…The Lord has given you the city! The city and everything in it must be totally destroyed as an offering to the Lord.' (Joshua 6: 16–17)

---

action point
Choose a war you know about and write *three* ways in which it fulfils the criteria for a just war listed opposite. Is there any way in which that war is unjust?

beware
Jihad is a Muslim's personal struggle against evil and not a 'holy war' as some people think. Sometimes jihad does involve armed struggle but it is in defence of the Muslim community.

exam watch
Many people would now say that World War II (1939–45) was a just war because Hitler had invaded other countries and had exterminated six million Jews.

Some conditions for a holy war (in the ancient Israelite thinking) include the following.

- It was what God wanted.
- God was in the midst of their armies as an unseen supreme commander.
- The losers were to be completely exterminated, including men, women and children.
- Victims of war and spoils were consecrated to God as though God's property.
- Anyone who kept some of the spoils would be stoned to death.

However, today there is no such idea in modern Jewish teaching.

There is no concept of a holy war in Islam, Hinduism, Buddhism or Sikhism.

> **beware**
> A holy war is not a war *between* religious traditions. The conflict between Roman Catholics and Protestants in Northern Ireland is *not* a holy war.

Religious teachings about war and peace

Christianity

- Killing is wrong: 'Do not commit murder.' (Exodus 20: 13)
- 'Love your neighbour as you love yourself.' (Matthew 22: 39)
- Jesus' teaching in the Sermon on the Mount not to take revenge, to love one's enemies, forgive others, turn the other cheek, and that those who work for peace are happy or blessed by God (Matthew 5); his temptations (Luke 4); his own example of non-retaliation at his arrest and death (Luke 22: 47–51).
- Quaker Peace Testimony (1660): 'We … testify to the world, that the spirit of Christ which leads us into all truth, will never move us to fight and war against any man with outward weapons, neither for the kingdom of Christ nor for the kingdoms of the world.'
- Most churches agree with the Roman Catholic position in *Gaudium et Spes*, which argues in favour of peace, the right to conscientious objection, use of resources to aid the poor rather than weapons, rooting out causes of injustice or war, condemnation of use of nuclear or other weapons of mass destruction, but as a last resort, the right of self-defence.
- The just war theory.
- In support of war: turning over tables of the moneychangers in the Temple, holy war ideas from the Old Testament.

Judaism

- In the struggle for a Jewish homeland, war is seen as a religious duty. For example, Joshua's battles.
- 'If a person intends to kill you, be the first to kill him.' (Talmud)
- Hopes for peace in Isaiah 2: 4 'They shall beat their swords into ploughshares, and their spears into pruning hooks: nation shall not take up sword against nation; they shall never again know war.' (the Jewish Bible)
- 'The world stands on three things, on justice, on truth and on peace.' (Ethics of the Fathers)
- Shalom (peace) is a Jewish greeting.

Islam

- Salaam, a Muslim greeting, means peace.
- The Qur'an teaches that you should aim to make peace and avoid war, but if that is impossible, once the war finishes you should 'make peace between them with justice and be fair: for Allah loves those who are fair.' (The Qur'an, surah 49: 9)
- The Qur'an teaches reconciliation and 'repel [evil] with what is better'. (The Qur'an, surah 41: 34)
- 'Hate your enemy mildly; he may become your friend one day.' (Hadith)

Hinduism

- Principle of ahimsa (not harming other creatures) balanced against dharma (duty).
- The Bhagavad Gita tells the story of Arjuna's dilemma as he faces battle and Krishna's teaching that he should fulfil his dharma by fighting: 'For a warrior, nothing is higher than a war against evil.' (Bhagavad Gita 2: 33) The warrior's dharma is to fight and by devotion to this duty he can attain perfection.

Buddhism

- Peace and compassion are the highest goals.
- Violence harms both victim and those doing the violence as it destroys inner peace.
- 'All (wars) stem from our lack of human understanding, of mutual trust, and of mutual respect, based on kindness and love for all beings.' (The Dalai Lama)
- A man is not great because he is a warrior and kills other men, but if he does not hurt any living being he is truly called a great man. (Dhammapada 270)
- 'Buddhism aims at creating a society where…one who conquers himself is more respected than those who conquer millions by military and economic warfare.' (Walpola Rahula, Sri Lankan Buddhist monk)

Sikhism

- The first Sikh community was committed to strict pacifism. Later, kirpan, originally a sword used in self-defence, came to symbolize dignity and self-respect, and the need to defend individuals' religious freedom.
- 'The Khalsa (pure ones) shall rule, no hostile powers shall exist…Those who enter the Khalsa for shelter will be protected. Without power, justice does not flourish, without justice everything is crushed and ruined.' (Dasam Granth)
- 'When all other means have failed, it is permissible to draw the sword.' (Guru Gobind Singh)
- Peace, however, is a gift of God. Prayers in Adi Granth: 'the Lord is a haven of peace.'

key ideas

Peace is not just the absence of war. Many people find inner peace, happiness and security through their religious faith.

Justice, bringing about what is right and fair, according to the law, and making up for what has been done wrong, is often used to argue for military action.

Sanctity of life, the belief that life is a precious gift from God and therefore sacred and worthy of the highest respect, is used by many to oppose killing in war, but some also use it to argue that it is right to save the lives of innocent victims, showing respect for life.

Short questions

a What does a pacifist believe about war? (2 marks) (AQA, 2002)

b Explain the terms 'justice' and 'sanctity of life'. (2 marks) (NEAB, 1999)

c Explain how a believer might use the idea of the 'sanctity of life' to argue that war is wrong. (4 marks) (AQA, 2002)

d State what is meant by 'just war' and 'holy war'. (2 marks) (NEAB, 2000)

Examination type questions

a Give an account of the work of *one* religious believer who has worked for peace or led non-violent protest. (4 marks) (AQA, 2002)

b 'Nuclear war can never be justified, no matter what the circumstances.' Do you agree? Give reasons for your answer, showing that you have thought about more than one point of view. Refer to religious teachings in your answer. (5 marks) (NEAB, 2000)

Student's answer

a *Martin Luther King protested against the racist laws in America. He made a famous speech ('I have a dream'), which talked about his hopes that one day his children would be judged by their character and not their colour. He thought everyone should be equal. In the end, he was shot dead.*

b *I agree. Nuclear war would kill millions of innocent people and destroy most of the countries where the war was taking place. What would be the point? What would anybody win? Just a destroyed planet and everyone dead. But I can also see why atomic bombs were dropped on Japan in World War II because that ended the war more quickly so lives could be saved. So maybe it is not that bad after all.*

Examiner's comments

a The student did not say *how* Martin Luther King protested, merely that he did. Only one reference was made to King's work: making a famous speech. However, the student did show some knowledge of its content. The rest of the answer, while true, did not provide enough detailed knowledge of his work.

Mark: 2/4

b The student correctly identifies the effects of a nuclear war: destruction of innocent lives and the environment, and the fact that no one can 'win', but should have said that this goes against the just war theory and explained how. They touch on an example of a different view but there is little reasoned argument nor is there a religious perspective.

Mark: 3/5

Examination practice

Read the article below.

> **MASSACRE!**
>
> The only people in the village were old men, women and children. Soldiers went through each house killing everyone they found …

a i Explain why a believer might say that the massacre described above was unjust. (2 marks) (AQA, 2002)
  ii Give *three* conditions of a just war. (3 marks) (AQA, 2002)

b Explain the teachings from *two* religious traditions which might influence attitudes about war. Name *each* tradition. (6 marks) (AQA, 2002)

c How might believers put these teachings into practise? (4 marks) (AQA, 2002)

d 'War is always wrong because innocent people are killed.' How far do you agree? Give reasons for your answer, showing that you have thought about more than one point of view. Refer to religious teachings in your answer. (5 marks) (AQA, 2002)

Checklist for revision

	Understand and know	Need more revision	Do not understand
I know the reasons used by religious believers for pacifism.	☐	☐	☐
I know the reasons used by religious believers for taking part in war.	☐	☐	☐
I know about the work of a religious believer who has worked for peace or led non-violent protest.	☐	☐	☐
I understand the criteria for a just war and I can explain why *one* war is just.	☐	☐	☐
I understand the concept of a holy war and I can give an example.	☐	☐	☐
I know what *two* religions teach about war and peace.	☐	☐	☐
I know *two* sacred texts or statements by religious authorities about war or peace from each of *two* religions.	☐	☐	☐
I can explain how the teachings are put into practise.	☐	☐	☐
I understand the meaning of:			
• peace	☐	☐	☐
• justice	☐	☐	☐
• sanctity of life.	☐	☐	☐
I understand how these ideas are important in discussions about war and peace.	☐	☐	☐

SECTION B: THINKING ABOUT MORALITY

11 The natural world

What do I need to know?

- Reasons why religious believers should care for the environment and promote its conservation.
- Conflicts that can arise for religious believers between uses of land and water (including destruction of natural habitats).
- Differing religious responses to animal rights and the means of protecting those rights.
- Differing religious responses to **vegetarianism**.
- Application of sacred texts, religious principles and statements by religious authorities to the environment and animal life.
- Concepts of responsibility, stewardship, creation, and sanctity of life.

hints and tips

In this section you must refer to *two* religious traditions, one of which must be Christianity.

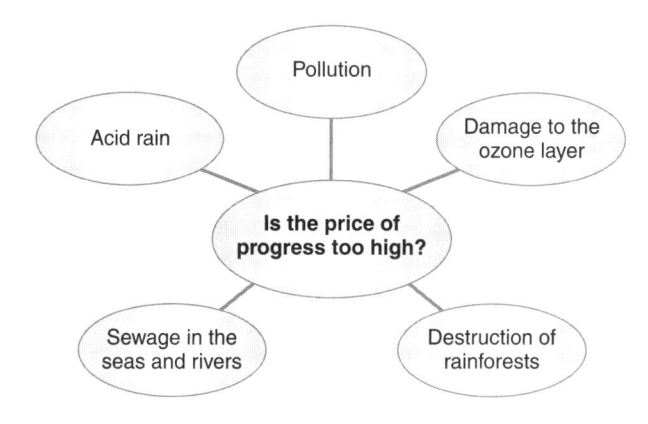

Is the price of progress too high?
- Pollution
- Acid rain
- Damage to the ozone layer
- Sewage in the seas and rivers
- Destruction of rainforests

hints and tips

You should study some of these problems in greater depth.

The conflict for religious believers includes:

- developing countries need foreign investment and income raised from selling products from the rainforests
- progress versus conservation
- decreasing production harms people's living standards by denying them jobs – who are we to demand such a sacrifice?
- the needs of people versus the good of the environment.

Religious believers argue that richer nations must help the rainforest countries to manage the forests without over-exploitation and give them money to help people whose livelihoods would be threatened.

action point

Find out *why* the tropical rainforests are being destroyed. How does burning the trees affect the environment?

Reasons to care for the environment and promote its conservation

- All religions agree that nature and life on earth must be respected and that people have a responsibility to care for animals and the environment.

55

- All religions (except Buddhism) believe in the creation of the world by God.
- Christians, Jews and Muslims believe that life is a sacred gift from God (sanctity of life) and that humans have been put in charge of the creation to look after it on God's behalf (stewardship/trusteeship). We have a responsibility to protect the environment and respond to its needs.
- Jews believe they have a duty to 'repair the world' (tikkun olam) by preventing **pollution** and not wasting resources.
- Muslims say nature is carefully balanced so we must use scarce resources, such as water, like good stewards (khalifah), replant trees, and so on.
- Hindus and Buddhists believe we are part of nature and should live in harmony with it rather than control it. Harmlessness (ahimsa) and compassion are key ideas.
- Sikhs believe people must respect God's creation and take responsibility for the needs of future generations.

Religious teachings about the environment and animal life

Christianity

- 'Then the Lord God placed the man in the Garden of Eden to cultivate it and guard it.' (Genesis 2: 15) Creation by God and idea of stewardship.
- 'The world and all that is in it belong to the Lord.' (Psalm 24: 1)
- Roman Catholic bishops (1971) criticized the rich nations' exploitation of natural resources and dumping of waste. The Pope (1988) called for a balanced policy between using and conserving the natural world and planning for the needs of future generations.
- The Church of England (1992) urged the government to take steps to establish a fair and economical use of the earth's resources and to reduce the impact of pollution and damage to plants and animals so people could live in harmony with nature.
- Quakers (the Society of Friends) believe that environmental issues are linked to poverty, abuse of human rights, and exploitation. In the eighteenth century, John Woolman said that the produce of the earth was a gift from God and to ruin the earth in the present day just to show 'outward greatness' would be an injury to the next generation.

Judaism

- 'Then the Lord God placed the man in the Garden of Eden to cultivate it and guard it.' (Genesis 2: 15) Creation by God and idea of stewardship.
- 'The world and all that is in it belong to the Lord.' (Psalm 24: 1)
- The Bible says to let the land rest from being planted every seventh year to allow it to recover and advises that fruit trees must not be cut down in time of war so that when peace returns, people can resume their life on the land.
- 'We have a responsibility to life, to defend it everywhere, not only against our own sins but also against those of others. We are all passengers together in this same fragile and glorious world.' (Jewish declaration at Assisi)

Islam

- Allah created everything: 'He has given you the earth for your heritage.' (The Qur'an, surah 6: 165)
- The earth is not ours but Allah's: 'To Him belongs all that is in the heavens and the earth.' (The Qur'an, surah 2: 256–7)
- People have the role of guardians (khalifah) and will be held accountable on the Day of Judgement.
- 'We are not masters of this earth; it does not belong to us to do what we wish. It belongs to God and He has entrusted us with its safekeeping…His trustees are responsible for maintaining the unity of His creation…its wildlife and natural environment.' (Muslim declaration at Assisi)

Hinduism

- Nature is sacred. It is part of the creator God, Brahma, and therefore deserves reverence.
- Harmlessness (ahimsa): avoid harming any living thing.
- The universe has been given in trust to people for their enjoyment.
- The human race is not separate from nature. People must 'halt the present slide towards destruction…to reverse the suicidal course upon which we have embarked…The earth is our mother, and we are all her children.' (Hindu declaration at Assisi)

Buddhism

- Harmlessness (ahimsa): avoid harming any living thing.
- One of the Five Precepts: avoid taking life and show loving kindness (metta) and compassion to all creatures.
- The law of karma: thoughts and actions have consequences, so our attitude towards nature is important.
- Monks and nuns may not 'destroy any plant or tree'. (Vinaya Pitaka)
- 'Buddhism is a religion of love, understanding and compassion, and committed towards the ideal of non-violence…it also attaches great importance to wildlife and the protection of the environment on which every being in this world depends for survival.' (Buddhist declaration at Assisi)

Sikhism

- 'The Lord pervades all created beings; God creates all and assigns all their tasks.' (Adi Granth 434)
- 'Sikhism teaches both respect and responsibility towards God's creation and the needs of future generations.' (Indarjit Singh JP, Editor, *Sikh Messenger*)
- The natural world is where each species follows its inner law (dharma) and subsequently will be judged in God's court.
- Human beings are custodians of God's creation (stewardship).

The rights and protection of animals

- 'Natural law' claimed animals had no soul, therefore had no rights.
- Animals are part of God's creation and humans have been put in charge of them (stewardship) so must take responsibility for them.
- God saw that the creation was 'good' so animals should not be forced to live unnaturally.

- Compassion must be shown to animals, a part of God's creation.
- Domestic animals can have a day of rest on the Sabbath.
- Animals are killed for meat according to strict rules (shechita). They are blessed, then killed as quickly and painlessly as possible.
- Jews disapprove of hunting, even for a living.
- The Rabbis taught that you should not buy an animal unless you could properly provide for it; it is wrong to blemish, injure or cause it distress.

- Legal rights for animals have existed since the thirteenth century.
- Muslims should only kill animals for food, not sport.
- Animals should not be kept in cages as it is unnatural and goes against the spirit of Islam.
- Killing animals for meat is strictly controlled (halal). The animal must be treated with respect, put at its ease, and killed quickly and painlessly 'in the name of Allah, the merciful, the compassionate' (The Qur'an).
- The principle of tawhid (the unity of God) links all living things together and requires respect shown to them.
- On the Day of Judgement a person may be condemned for mistreating animals.

- One of five daily duties of the householder is to make offerings to all creatures – put food outside the home.
- Humans are related to animals by the process of rebirth (samsara). You may be reborn as an animal.
- Many deities appear as animals.
- Cows are sacred in India – a symbol of the harmless quality of life.
- 'No person should kill animals helpful to all. Rather by serving them, one should attain happiness.' (Yajurveda 13: 47)

- Practice of non-violence (ahimsa) and compassion (metta) towards all life.
- Animals are like people: they have feelings, avoid suffering and seek happiness.
- Animals have their own right to exist; they should be respected and preserved for that reason, not just because they are useful to us.
- 'However mean, however small, the animal may seem, life to that animal is as important and precious as it is to us.' (John Bowker, *Worlds of Faith*)

- Sikhs must be kind to people, animals and birds.
- If used for food, animals should be killed quickly and painlessly at a single stroke.
- Sikhs are forbidden to eat meat killed by Jewish or Muslim ritual slaughter, which they see as cruel.
- There are no strict food laws, although many Sikhs are vegetarian, but out of consideration for their Hindu neighbours, most will not eat beef.

Vegetarianism

Many people are vegetarians for moral reasons.

- It is wrong to kill animals.
- Farming methods (battery hens), transport of animals, and methods of slaughter are cruel or unnatural.
- People are starving in the developing world, yet 90 per cent of agricultural land is used for cattle food instead of food for humans.
- Ten times more people can be sustained on a vegetarian diet than on meat.

Christians, Jews, Muslims and Sikhs do not *have* to be vegetarians, but *may be* for moral reasons or because of their religion's teaching about creation.

Hindus and Buddhists are mainly vegetarian but Buddhists will eat meat if necessary for their health, if there is no alternative, or if they will offend someone by not doing so.

Practical application of teachings

Ways a believer might put the teachings of their religious tradition into practise:

- working on practical conservation projects
- campaigning for particular issues
- vegetarianism/other personal choices which preserve some aspect of the environment; for example, limiting one's use of the car
- prayer/meditation/raising consciousness.

Short questions		
a	State *two* ways in which the environment is being damaged.	(2 marks) (NEAB, 2000)
b	Why are some religious believers vegetarians?	(2 marks) (AQA, 2002)
c	Describe *two* ways in which religious believers could care for the environment.	(4 marks) (AQA, 2002)

Examination type questions

a i Explain the terms 'sanctity of life' and 'stewardship'. (2 marks) (NEAB, 1999)
   ii How might Christians apply *each* of these ideas to arguments about the right and wrong use of natural resources? (8 marks) (NEAB, 1999)

Student's answer

a i Sanctity of life means that life is given to us by God. Stewardship means we have to take care of God's world for him.
   ii Christians would apply 'sanctity of life' by saying that we must not destroy life because it was given by God. It is not up to us to take life, it is up to God. They would say that it is wrong to destroy animals for no reason because they are God's creatures. We can use animals for food because human life is sacred, but we are wrong to kill endangered species just for a fur coat. They would use 'stewardship' to say that the world does not really belong to us but to God. We are only looking after it and we should keep it in good condition for God. When we waste natural resources, we are wasting something that is not really ours. We will have to answer to God if we pollute the planet through our negligence and greed.

Examiner's comments

a i Correct definitions. Mark: 2/2
   ii The candidate applies the terms correctly in each case and relates the concepts to arguments about the right or wrong use of natural resources, giving examples. 'Stewardship' also mentions accountability and causes (negligence and greed) of pollution. Mark: 8/8

Examination practice

Read the newspaper headline below.

> **PROPOSED NEW ROAD CAUSES LOCAL PROTEST**
>
> Community split over building of by-pass

a Explain *one* reason why a religious believer might support the building of the new road. (2 marks) (AQA, 2002)

b Give *three* examples of how natural habitats are being destroyed. (3 marks) (AQA, 2002)

c Explain the teachings of *two* religious traditions which might influence attitudes about the use of the earth's resources. (6 marks) (AQA, 2002)

d How might believers put these teachings into practise? (4 marks) (AQA, 2002)

e 'God created the world, so God should take care of it.' Do you agree? Give reasons for your answer, showing that you have thought about more than one point of view. Refer to religious teachings in your answer. (5 marks) (AQA, 2002)

11 The natural world

Checklist for revision

	Understand and know	Need more revision	Do not understand
I know reasons why religious believers in *two* religions should care for the environment.	☐	☐	☐
I understand the moral dilemmas over the use of land and water.	☐	☐	☐
I know the attitudes to animal rights in *two* religious traditions.	☐	☐	☐
I know the religious attitudes to vegetarianism in *two* religious traditions.	☐	☐	☐
I know what *two* religions teach about the natural world.	☐	☐	☐
I can explain how the teachings are put into practise.	☐	☐	☐
I understand the meaning of:			
• responsibility	☐	☐	☐
• stewardship	☐	☐	☐
• creation	☐	☐	☐
• sanctity of life.	☐	☐	☐
I understand how these ideas are important in discussions about the natural world.	☐	☐	☐

Glossary

Absolute morality The belief that what is morally right and wrong applies to all circumstances at all times

Agnostic Someone who believes that it is impossible to know whether God exists

Atheist Someone who believes that God does not exist and that it is meaningless to claim there is a God

Big Bang A scientific theory about how the universe came into existence

Charismatic worship (Christian) Filled with and led by the Holy Spirit

Commitment (in marriage) Taking vows to be faithful to one's partner for life

Community A group of people who share common values and feel responsible for each other

Compassion Literally 'suffering with' others; feeling sorry for someone who is suffering and wanting to help them

Conscience A sense of right and wrong; a feeling of guilt when doing wrong

Contract (in marriage) A formal agreement or legal bond between the couple

Conversion Change of belief

Covenant (in marriage) A binding or lifelong agreement before God

Creation The act of causing something to exist; the religious view that God made the universe

Design argument The argument for God's existence based on the intricacy, beauty and interdependence of life and the universe

Discrimination Acting on prejudice (for example, stopping someone from doing something because of their race, colour, religion, gender, and so on)

Equality Everyone having the same human rights

Evolution Theory that human life developed from single celled creatures by a process of natural selection and adaptation to the environment

First Cause The argument that, since everything has a cause, God is the first cause of the universe

Free will The ability to choose or decide one's own actions

General revelation Knowing God through nature or ordinary, common human experiences

Holy war A war fought in the name of God and with a religious purpose

Immanent (about God's nature) That God is present in and involved with the universe and life on earth

Impersonal (about God's nature) That God is not a 'person' but perhaps more like a force or some other idea in people's minds

Justice Bringing about what is legally right and fair or making up for what has been done wrong

Glossary

Just war A war that meets the conditions that are said to justify military action against another country

Meditation Focusing on God usually through silent reflection

Monotheism Belief in one God

Pacifism A belief that all violence is wrong (shown in the refusal to fight in a war)

Personal (about God's nature) That God is someone with 'human' characteristics with whom people can have a relationship

Pollution Harm caused to the natural world often by chemical waste from industry

Polytheism Belief in more than one God

Prayer Communicating with God

Prejudice Pre-judging someone on the basis of a stereotype

Quality of life Not merely being alive, but living without excessive suffering; able to experience life and communicate with others

Reason A source of moral authority; a person's mind working out what is right or wrong by thinking through the consequences of the action

Relative morality What is morally right and wrong varies and depends on the individual circumstances

Religious experience The direct and personal experience of the reality of God or of a spiritual truth

Responsibility Being accountable for one's own actions; a duty to care for others

Sacrament An outward (religious) action, which gives a spiritual blessing to those involved

Sacramental ritual (or worship) A religious ceremony in which a sacrament is celebrated

Sanctity of life Idea that life is sacred because it is given by God and should not be ended by human beings

Scripture The holy writings or sacred books of a religion

Sources of moral authority The things that guide religious believers in moral decision making, that is, scripture, tradition, reason, conscience and religious leaders

Special revelation God making himself known through direct, personal experience or an unusual, specific event

Stewardship Being responsible and looking after something on behalf of another (for example, humans caring for the created world on behalf of God)

Theist A person who believes that God exists

Tradition A world religion or denomination of Christianity; a source of moral authority

Transcendent (about God's nature) That God is beyond and outside the universe and life on earth

Vegetarianism The belief that it is wrong to kill animals and fish for food

Index

abortion 25, 27–31
absolute morality 25, 28, 33
adultery 32–3, 34
agnostics 6, 10
animals 55, 58–9
atheists 6, 10

charity 43–7
conscience 25–6, 28, 48
contraception 33–4, 36–7
creation 6–9, 15

decision making 25–6
design of universe 8–9, 11
discrimination 38–42, 49
divorce 34–5

environment 55–7, 60
equality 38–42
evil 9, 10, 15, 18–20, 48
evolution 6, 8–9
existence of God 6–12

first cause 6
free will 15, 18–19

human nature 18–19

justice 13, 38–9, 43, 48, 49–50, 52

karma 15, 16, 18
knowing God 9–10, 22–4

love 10, 13, 21, 35–6, 39, 40, 43

marriage 9, 32–7
meditation 10, 11
monotheism 21, 22
moral authority 25–6

nature of God 13, 19, 21–4

peace 48, 52
personal God 7, 10, 21–2
polytheism 22
poverty 43–7
power of God 13, 19, 21
prayer 10, 11
prejudice 38–42, 49

relative morality 25, 28
religious experience 9–11, 22–3
revelations 9, 21, 22–3

sanctity of life 27–9, 52, 56
scientific theories 6, 8
sex 32–4, 37
sin 15, 18, 19
stewardship 43, 56
suffering 13–17, 19

theists 6, 11

universe creation 6–9

war 48–54
worship 9–11, 22